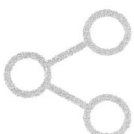

HOW TO ADVERTISE LIKE A
SOCIAL MEDIA AGENCY

ODOLENA KOSTOVA

Copyright © 2018 Odolena Digital
All rights reserved.

ISBN-9781718818866

DEDICATION

To my beloved Vitali Mueller who encouraged me to write this book and supported me while writing.
Thank you for being on my side!

CONTENTS

Introduction 7
    Get in touch 10
    Why I wrote this book 12
    The Problem with Agencies 13
    The Problem With In-House Marketing 13
    The problem with the internet marketing gurus 14
1. Determine your marketing Goal 16
    See, Think, Do, Care 17
2. Google Search Ads 20
    Google's auction Explained 22
    What makes a good quality score? 24
    How to calculate an optimal profitable cost per click? 25
    GLOSSARY: 27
3. Your First Campaign In Google Ads 29
    New interface vs old interface 29
    Networks 31
    Location and Languages 32
    Budget 33
    Bidding Strategies 34
    Dynamic Ads 39
    Audiences 40
    Extensions 42
    Ad rotation 46
    Campaign URL Options 46
    Ad groups 50
4. Generating Keywords 52

What exactly is a keyword? 52

Keywords Matches 53

Negative Keywords 55

How to find negative keywords? 57

    Search term report 57

    The Overview Report 59

How to select great keywords? 59

    Keyword Research 63

    Google Trends 64

    SEMrush 68

    SmiliarWeb 70

5. Creating ads 72

What is the essential goal of an ad? 72

Your Headline 74

Taking your ad copy to the next level 76

6. Landing Pages (Bonus) 81

7. Mobile Search Marketing 90

AMP (Accelerated Mobile Pages) 95

8. Facebook Advertising 100

Very brief history of Facebook 100

Facebook Business Manager 105

Facebook Pixel 107

Offline events 110

Brand Safety 110

9. Creating your first facebook campaign 113

Objectives 114

Ad sets in Facebook 117

Audiences 120

Facebook ads 124

10. The Google Display Network 130
    What is the Google Display Network? 130
    Creating a GDN Campaign 131
    Ad Rotation 133
    Frequency 133
    Content exclusions 135
11. Audiences On Google Display 137
    Affinity audiences and Custom Affinity 138
    In-Market Segments and Custom Intent 139
    How to check what Google thinks you are interested in? 145
    Remarketing and Similar Audience 150
    Creating an audience in Google Analytics 155
    Other display targeting 160
    Creating Responsive Display Ads 164
    Finalising your campaign 166
19. Advertising on youtube 168
    Why should you consider YouTube? 169
    YouTube Ad Formats 169
    YouTube Marketing Metrics 181
    YouTube Analytics 182
    Make the Ultimate True View Video Creative 184
    Building Your YouTube Campaign 188
    YouTube Remarketing 193
13. Gmail Advertising 195
    Set up a Gmail Campaign 196
Final Words 200

INTRODUCTION

This book is written with the intention to make online advertising easy and understandable for someone who wants to run their own campaigns with the quality of a marketing agency.

Online advertising is becoming more and more simplified, but still it can be confusing for a beginner.

In this book you will learn how to practically run ads on some of the most popular channels: Facebook and Google.

Who can benefit from this book?

This book is perfect for someone who is starting a business, advertises affiliate products or just wants to enhance their skills. This can be the foundation of a career change or even making your own marketing consultancy. These are some of the people, I had in mind when writing this book:

- Advertising Manager
- Business owner

- Entrepreneur
- Social media consultant
- Affiliate Marketer
- Marketing consultant
- Pay per click specialist
- Marketing Manager
- What is inside?

1. Determine your marketing goal

Lays out a framework which will help you define your marketing objectives. This is a starting point of defining for what purpose you will use the technical skills you are going to get in the following chapters.

2. Google Search Ads

You will learn how the **online auction** works, what is a **Quality Score** and how to **calculate profitable cost per click**. You will also get a very useful glossary of some of the most commonly user terms.

3. Your First Campaign in Google Ads

Introduces the different campaign settings and how to avoid common mistakes. We will also go through **each of the bidding strategies** – manual and automated. Then, we will talk about audiences on search and specifically **Remarketing Lists for Search Ads (RLSA)**. Finally, you will learn the purpose of **Ad Groups** and how to organise them correctly.

4. Generating Keywords

Presents the **different match types, negative keywords** and how to use them to stay relevant with your ads. The chapter goes on with some tips to do **keyword research** with tools like the **Keyword Planner and Google Trends**.

5. Creating Ads

This chapter introduces some of the most important ad types like **Extended Text ads, Responsive ads for Search, keyword insertions, customizers and Dynamic Ads** in more detail.

6. Landing pages – Bonus

This chapter is giving some best practices when it comes to creating a high-converting landing page.

7. Mobile Search marketing

You will learn about some useful tools to measure the performance of your website on mobile devices. Also it covers the basics of **AMP (Accelerated Mobile Pages)**

8. Facebook Advertising.

The chapter gives an overall history of the development of Facebook and its other platforms. You will learn about **Facebook Business Manager**, how to set up **Facebook Pixel**, how to track offline events and use settings to protect your brand.

9. Creating your first Facebook campaign.

Guides through the setup of a campaign, **Facebook audiences** and the different ad formats.

10. The Google Display Network

Reviews the main differences and similarities between Facebook and GDN in a step by step guide to create a Google Display campaign.

11. Audiences on Google Display

Examines the different audiences from Google, explaining how they are formed. You will learn how to track what data Google collects about your online behaviour to offer the most relevant ads.

12. Advertising on YouTube

Presents YouTube advertising techniques and ways of **measuring performance**. You will understand the **different ad formats** and how you are charged for each type.

13. Gmail Advertising

Deconstructs the campaign set up, targeting opportunities, ad formats and measurement on Gmail.

To access the 24 marketing tactics go to Odolena.com/twenty-four-tactics and get your free copy.

Get in touch

If you want to **leave me feedback**, please do by emailing odolena.digital@odolena.com I really believe that this book can help businesses set up their advertising campaigns and improve performance. I also understand there would be things which you might to know more about. Your feedback means a lot to me, as I would like to know if there is any way I could improve.

Are you interested in working with me?

Businesses hire me to help them with:

1. Creating and Managing Their Online Campaigns

I can help your business by creating Google Ads and Facebook Ads campaigns from scratch or optimise and fully manage existing channels. Your goal might be:

- Brand awareness for a new product
- Generating leads for B2B or B2C
- Getting more mobile app installs from Google Play or the App Store
- More online purchases from your website

2. Educating and Training Their Teams

If you have a team already, but you want education for them, this is something I would love to help with! I can create and present at your office a customized full-day or half-day course on topics like:

Beginner level

- Google Ads Fundamental Knowledge
- Selling Digital Services
- Facebook Ads Fundamentals

Intermediate level

- Marketing Automation and Smart Bidding with Google Ads
- Google Display Audiences
- Shopping Campaigns with Google Ads and Shopify
- YouTube for Performance Marketing
- Attribution Modelling and Conversion Tracking

I can also create longer courses with a specific focus depending on the business' needs.

To get a quote, please email me a brief intro to your business and your requirements at Odolena.digital@odolena.com

Why I wrote this book

During the last year and a half, I have been regularly publishing articles on the subject of digital marketing. Becoming visible online is a topic which I have been fascinated with. The variety of opportunities and new platforms is becoming more and more incredible every day. From my experience, even people who are very active online as users are taking advantage of only 1% of the full capacity of the platforms available to them. Businesses still shy away from being too active and open with their brand story online. These are missed opportunities which make me upset.

I first started working in digital marketing in 2012 with the Google Digital Garage. This initiative of Google has the purpose of helping small U.K. businesses to use the tools available to them like Google AdWords and Google My Business(formerly Google Business Locations). Visiting small business owners and talking to them made me aware of how access to relevant information and tools can really impact a local enterprise.

Since then, I have been working as a Global Search Engine Marketing Manager for a large company, running Google Ads campaigns in multiple international markets. I have also been consulting medium-sized and small businesses on how to expand their online reach with digital marketing.

I realised that often business owners lack confidence in online marketing. Many of them feel they need to outsource their marketing to an agency or a freelancer to which they half-trust.

Having a well-trained, experienced in-house team is a luxury even for some well-funded start-ups or medium-sized businesses.

The Problem with Agencies

I know a business owner whose company is booming. On the surface they appear to be small, but when it comes to revenue, they are getting bigger and bigger. She now wants to increase her advertising spend on Google Ads. Until now they have trusted a small advertising agency, which has brought excellent results, but charged almost 40% of the ad spend in fees. On top of that, the agency does not really take any initiative – the ads and the campaigns are the same since they were set up. Since, my friend's company is one of the lower spending customers in the agency's portfolio, her account is not a priority..

Even with an increased budget for advertising her company, she will still be in the lower division of the agency's portfolio. Compared to any larger business even £20-30k advertising spend per month is tiny. On top of that comes the hefty 30-40% agency fee.

Small agencies focus on getting as many small clients as possible and charge a higher percent on low spending clients to make a profit. They do not take the time to deeply understand the needs of each business and work with a "cookie-cutter" approach.

What if there was a way to learn everything you need to know about online marketing, without reading many contradicting books and visiting tons of blogs with outdated information? What if all you ever needed to know was in one short book?

The Problem With In-House Marketing

Having an in-house team of marketers is amazing, but not affordable to small businesses. Specialists in digital marketing are in very high demand and are paid relatively high wages. If you are start-up or you are just trying to prove a product concept, you would not hire a whole team to run ads for you.

You can start yourself and once you have a proven concept, then gradually expand and bring in people in to run your ads for you.

But how do you start?

This is why I brought this book out. It is for people who would like to run ads but have no option to hire an agency or their own marketing team. By following what I am going to teach in this book you will be able to create profitable online campaigns at the level of an agency.

The problem with the internet marketing gurus

Then there are those of you who have been searching for ways to scale up their affiliate marketing business. You have watched every guru on the internet, purchased so many courses which teach contradicting information and spent so much money on errors.

Technology changes so quickly and newest products from Google and Facebook are usually made available to the big adverting spenders. Marketing gurus have access to all the Betas ad versions before everyone else. Suddenly you realize that to recreate their marketing you need a professional design team and camera crew.

The problem with the gurus is that they are extremely successful. This is a contradicting thought, but I will show you what I mean.

When you spend a few million dollars on YouTube ads annually, you have a team of account managers from YouTube who will come to your office and help you create the best ad possible. They will bring in data from thousands of advertisers knowing what works.

I am not saying that what gurus preach is not true. The difference is that everything they share with you is just enough to get you to buy their next product. They are rich and have a professional marketing team and personal account managers from Facebook, Google and Twitter who help them with their campaigns. They probably have paid some of the top professionals in the field to consult them and make sure their marketing is winning.

You can try and mimic what they do. This is a good strategy, but only if you understand the newest technology and how to use it.

This book is a straightforward guide on how to run campaigns for someone who would like to promote their business online. No matter whether you own a product, do arbitrage sales, affiliate marketing, drop-shipping, the strategies I teach in this book will help you increase sales, build brand awareness and break out of obscurity.

1. DETERMINE YOUR MARKETING GOAL

Determine your goal – is it lead generation, sales, improving brand awareness or all of them at once? A business can have several different revenue streams and different needs for each of them. Each platform online has tools for expanding reach or focusing on the audience which is most likely to convert.

A full marketing strategy often comprises of various goals in the different stages of the funnel.

What do I mean by funnel?

You have probably heard people talking about marketing funnels. The word has been used with completely different meanings. To avoid confusion, I am talking about the different stages of interest through which a potential customer goes from before knowing about your product to completing a purchase. At each stage you are getting the customer closer and closer to the desired action you want them to take. Let's see how this works with a simple framework, created by Google for marketers.

See, Think, Do, Care – a Framework by Google

This is a framework created by Google for marketers to distinguish the different stages of interest of online users at each stage of the funnel. The idea is that at every stage users leave signals online. You can read these signals and understand how interested they are, how much they know about your brand or the market in general and how likely they are to buy.

See

The first stage is called "See" and has to do with your brand visibility. One of the biggest problems for any business, if not the biggest is getting out of obscurity. We live in a very competitive economy. Making your product visible to the right people is the first and most important challenge you must overcome.

At this stage your potential customers might not be aware of your brand and might not even be aware of the type of product you are selling. They still leave some signals they could be your potential customers. These might be what type of videos they watch on YouTube, websites they spend time on, apps they download as well as searches on Google.

Advertising platforms collect these signals and create audiences based on interests you can target. At this stage, you can make brand awareness campaigns on YouTube, Facebook and the Google Display Network targeting a wide audience with interest or likelihood to be interested. Each of these channels has a solution built precisely for solving a visibility problem. I will go through each of them in the following chapters.

Think

These are people who have some intent to buy, but not urgently. They have been on your website but, have not bought or converted. This is very normal – only 2% of customers convert on the first point of interaction. This is why you must learn to follow up with them. Remarketing is one of the best ways of reaching to these people.

You can define groups of web visitors by the pages they have visited in a considerable precision. At this stage you are working with lists of prospects who are anonymous. Google, Facebook and other platforms collect data related to the device and internet protocol address of these people, but nothing that gives away their personality. It can be anything from people visiting your site, choosing to see a full YouTube ad, reading your blog, etc.

How remarketing works is in a very general sense you collect anonymous data about your website visitors, YouTube watchers, etc. and then show your ads to these people on the internet while they are doing something else.

At this stage you must constantly remind the customer about your existence. Some businesses are afraid of getting too annoying by constantly showing their ads. Believe me, the number of sales will outnumber the complaints.

Do

This is a stage when people have already commercial intent. Eventually, most of the people who are interested vaguely in your product will arrive to a point when they will buy. This can be remarketing to people who put items in a basket, but did not check out. Also, this can be traffic from people searching buy+ something in Google. At this stage, you might see people looking directly for your brand.

What is important here is that all your actions are optimized towards your most important financial KPI. Anything else would lead to over-optimization.

What it means is, that businesses should agree how important certain conversion is. What is the return on advertising spend? If you spend too much to acquire leads that do not convert or cheap product which does not bring revenue.

Care

This stage comes after someone has become a paying client. That's right, your marketing doesn't stop there! On the contrary, sold customers are a great source of new sales, recommendations and referral business.

If you are using some kind of customer relationship management platform (CRM) like Salesforce or an email automation software like MailChimp, for example, you have all your customer data there. Many CRMs have integrations with Google and Facebook and allow you show ads to lists of previous customers or subscribers, based on the data you have collected about them – name, email, address, etc.

Once you have determined what you want goal you want to focus on, start thinking of how your customers are more likely to find your product, do they search for it on Google, do they watch reviews, do they explore social media and which ones.

Then, let's dissect the channels one by one.

2. GOOGLE SEARCH ADS

This is great place to start for almost all types of businesses because you can find potential clients when they are most actively searching for your product or service. Different markets have specific most popular search engines. Google is the top SE in Europe, the Americas and Middle East. It is not available in China, but people still can access it through VPN (Virtual Private Network).

In some countries Google is available, but is just not that popular. If you happen to target these markets you might have to get familiar with local most popular search engines like Baidu in China, Yandex in Russia and Yahoo in Japan. In this book I will focus on

Google, as it is the leader of search engine innovation and advertising technology.

Map Of The Most Popular Websites Across The World

Google's advertising platform, Google Ads[1], allows marketing to customers based on search terms. Advertisers can choose words or phrases related to their product called "keywords". Whenever someone searches for a term which contains the keyword or part of it, there is an auction happening between businesses which are bidding on this keyword. Everyone who would like to show their ad in this unique search result sets a bid – the maximum they would like to pay when someone clicks on their ad. Bids can be manually chosen for every keyword you have.

Based on the bid and the quality of the ad they have, Google estimates which ads to appear, in what order and how much each advertiser will be charged if someone clicks on their ad this time. These auctions get performed thousands and thousands of times online – every time someone does a search. Remember, an advertiser is only charged, if someone clicks on their ad. Your ad can appear multiple times for free if no one is clicking on it.

---

[1] Recently rebranded to the more simple Google Ads. The rebranding was announced during the writing of this book, so both terms are used with equal meaning.

Google's auction Explained

Your goal is to get people to click on your ad – this is how you bring them to your website and have a chance to get them to subscribe, buy, fill out a form, etc.

Google's auction is different from a traditional auction where the highest bidder wins. It is called second-price auction, or an auction where the winner must only pay just the minimum to keep their position. This means no matter how much you decide to bid, you are most likely to pay less than your actual bid. There are a few key factors which determine the ad position – bid, keyword quality score and account history.

Here we introduce some new terms. I will explain Quality score in more detail, but for now think of it as a 10 to 1 mark from Google most of the keywords you are bidding on receives. Lowest score is 1 and highest is 10. There are three main factors which determine your score – landing page experience, expected click-through rate and ad relevance.

By multiplying the quality score and your bid Google estimates a rank for your ad. Let's imagine you are bidding 5 dollars for your keyword and your quality score for this keyword is 4 out of 10. Your ad rank will then be 20(5X4=20). In the auction, there is also someone else bidding on the same keyword, but only 4 dollars with a high-quality score - 7 out of 10. Then their ad rank will be 4X7=28. The advertiser with the highest rank takes position one and then every other advertiser takes the consecutive positions based on their rank. In our example, you get position 2, because your rank is 20 and the other advertiser will get position 1 because their rank is 28.

The Chief Economist of Google Hal Varian explains the Google Ads auction with a simple formula:

P1XQ1=B2XQ2

P1 = the price the first ranked advertiser will pay if someone clicks their ad

Q1= the quality score of the first ranked advertiser

B2 = the bid, or maximum amount advertiser 2 is ready to pay if someone clicks their ad. This is different from how much he actually pays!

Q2 =quality score of the second-ranked advertiser

To find the actual price advertiser one will be charged for a click we derive the following:

P1=(B2XQ2)/Q1

In our case:

P1=(4X5)/7

P1=$2.85

The advertiser with the highest rank was bidding $4 but ends up paying only $2.85 because of their high quality score.

And what about you? You were bidding much higher but could not get the first place because of your score. How much you will pay for a click depends on the next person in the auction – the third-ranked advertiser. Let's say they bid $6 and have a quality score of 3.

P2=(B3XQ3)/Q2

P2=(6X3)/4

P2=$4.5

You were biding $7 dollars, but ended up paying $4.5, however, the person above you was bidding $4 and ended up paying $2.85.

You might say it is not fair, but this is how Google selects only the most relevant and most useful ads. The reason why Google prefers advertisers with high quality scores and relevant ad extensions is simply because that provide a better experience for the users.

Besides the quality score, Google also takes into consideration the factor of extensions. Ad extensions like a phone number, location, sitelinks and promotions can help advertisers with lower quality score achieve better positions. The extension factor is not revealed to advertisers – there is no extension score you can see. Now Google takes into consideration 80% of the quality score factor and 20% of the ad extensions factor. The actual ad rank formula is:

Ad Rank=Max. CPC bid X (Quality scoreX0.8)+(ad extensionsX0.2)

In the example above we simplified this to:

Ad Rank=Max CPC bid X Quality Score

In general, the recommendation of Google is to have as many ad extensions as possible, because this helps your ad rank. In the following chapter when we write ad copy, I will go in detail about each of the ad extensions and how you can use it.

What makes a good quality score?

The precise formula by which Google determines a quality score is not publicly available. However, the main factors for a good quality score are clear.

Expected CTR – this is according to Google's Chief Economist, Hal Varian the Account history of performance – newer Google Ads accounts have more difficulty in getting top Quality score keywords. With time and most importantly more conversion data in the history, Google is more reassured about the reputation of this advertiser and the quality scores increase. The more conversions your website is getting the faster you will be able to get through the initial phase.

Ad relevance to the search query – This is one of the factors which advertisers can easily influence. If you are bidding on a certain keyword, you must have this keyword in your ad headline and preferable in the description. This makes your ad more relevant to what the user is trying to find information about and more likely that they click on it. Using something called ad customizers or dynamic ads can help you get your ad text to change depending on what the user is looking for.

Landing page experience and landing page relevance to the keyword. The landing page must provide a great experience – high loading speed, easy navigation and simple design. Mobile page experience is also essential for reaching a good quality score. Since recently Google introduced a Mobile Speed score for landing pages which you can see in a separate column in your account. I have dedicated a separate chapter only on mobile search. This is the direction all online advertising is taking at the moment, so it is absolutely crucial to pay attention to the mobile device experience of your users.

How to calculate an optimal profitable cost per click?

To estimate your acceptable average cost per click and run profitable campaigns you must know some figures about your business.

Conversion rate. Conversion rate is the ratio between people clicking on your website through ads and the ones of them who make a purchase, subscribe, or fill out a form to get more information.

Profit margin. Profit margin is a calculation of what is left after your production costs are taken out of your revenue and how much percent is this from the total revenue. If you are running a shoe factory, which costs you 40$ to make a shoe and when you sell this shoe for 80$, you have a 50% profit margin.

The most difficult part is the calculation is in **conversion value** or what a conversion is worth to you. In many cases this would be more of an approximation. If you are running e-commerce, for example, once acquired customer might turn into a regular. When searching for your brand next time they might click on your ad again. This will lead to additional costs of acquisition. Also, when it comes to e-commerce values we can use a term called **average order value.** You can calculate this if you divide the value of all orders by the number of individual buyers.

If you are collecting leads by using a form and providing some free information in exchange for the lead's contact details, then you can assign a **value to each lead**. You can do this by approximating how many of the leads you get end up buying from you and what is the average cost they end up paying.

One reliable way of calculating your CPC(cost per click) is this:

First, multiply the average cost a customer will pay(final sale or average order value) by the conversion rate to a sale(how many of the people who click on an ad become paying customers). This is the **unique value per website visit** from an ad. If you run a fashion company and your average customer pays $3000 for a suite. From a 1000 clicks you get one paying customer – 0.001 rate to a sale.

3000X0.001=3

This is the value of a unique visit to your website.

Let's say it costs you a $1000 to produce a suite. Your profit margin is then (3000-1000)/3000X100% = 66%. In this case you should not bid more than 66%X3=$1.97 and you will always remain profitable with your account.

If you are not directly selling, but collecting leads instead, you have to take into consideration two ratios. The click to become a lead ration(conversion through Google AdWords) and the lead to paid customer ratio. If you run an education company and you have a 10% conversion rate to a lead from your landing page. This means 100 out of 1000 people who click on your ad fill out a form on your website with their email and other personal information. Then out of these 100, let's say 10 ends up buying the education.

If your education costs $3000, then you must multiply this first by the click to lead ratio and then by the lead to paying customer ratio. So, you will get:

(3000x0.1)x0.1=30

This formula can help you estimate when it is profitable for you to run online campaigns not only on search engines but also social media and any other kind of pay per click channel.

GLOSSARY:

Keyword – combination of words, or one word which triggers an ad to appear after a search for this word or combination of words.

Click – an online user who saw your ad clicked on it. It does not mean they bought or subscribed, or did any desired action. In most cases you will pay per click.

Impression – your ad was shown to an online user who searched for a term close or identical to a keyword you are bidding on.

Click-through rate – clicks divided by impressions. Gives signal to Google

Bid – the maximum amount you would like to pay for click when someone searches a word or combination of words.

Ad rank – the position at which your ad appears in the search results, determined by an auction between the other advertisers bidding on the same keyword.

Quality score - score given by Google on every keyword. It is determined by a combination of the relevancy of the keyword to the ad copy, the URL and the landing page. Click-through rate is also a key component.

3. YOUR FIRST CAMPAIGN IN GOOGLE ADS

Creating a campaign in Google AdWords is not as simple as it may seem, but if you keep in mind a few rules I am going to share in the next chapters, you will be able to do this as well as any professional.

To set up your account, you must have an email from Google and any form of payment – credit, debit card or bank transfer.

There are only a few things you should bear in mind when creating an account as you will not be able to change these later – currency and time zone.

Everything else, including payment method, you can add later.

New interface vs old interface

Google has been gradually updating anew interface on Google AdWords which will eventually replace the old one. The new interface has still some flows which will with the time be removed, but it has the advantage to be quite fast and easy to navigate.

You also get a lot of useful graphs and recommendations you would normally not get from the old version.

As I would expect many of you are just starting now, I would recommend you use the new interface, as this would be the future of Google AdWords and the sooner you learn how to navigate in it, the better.

The old interface will look like this:

Figure 1 Google adwords - the old interface

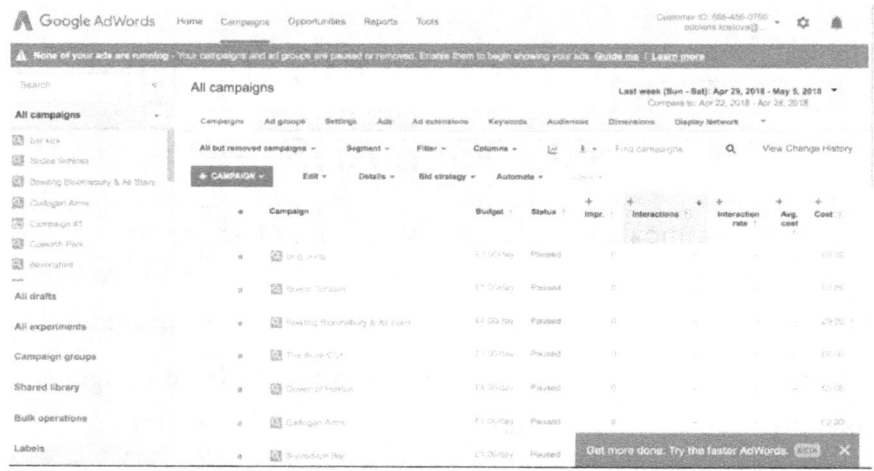

The blue tab in the lower right corner indicates the place where you can switch to the new interface. Which looks like this:

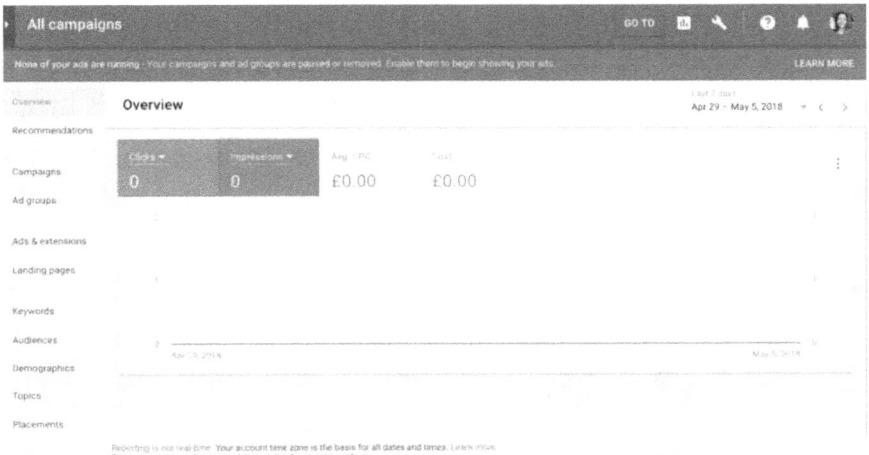

Your home page in the new Google AdWords Interface

Sometimes you are automatically logged in the new interface, but if you want to go back to the old one (while you still can) you can do this by clicking on the little wrench icon and selecting return to the old AdWords.

Setting up your first campaign is easy. Just go to the Campaigns tab and select the + sign in the new interface or the *Create a New Campaign* button in the old one. Then select search campaign type to start the setting up. In the new interface you can choose whether you would like to auto-optimise towards sales, leads or website traffic(clicks). You can select one of these options, but in this book, I will teach you how to do this manually so that you can select a campaign without a goal.

Networks

When setting up networks, Google will give you the option to choose between Search and Display Select. I don't recommend you

Display Select. This may result in extra costs and bad results. In this book we will set up a display campaign separately – step by step, so don't worry about this.

I would still recommend you to tick the box under Search and enable Google's Search Partners. This will allow your ad to show on some smaller search engines like Ask Jeeves, for example. You can later track the results you get from these networks and decide whether to keep them or not. However, this option will allow your ad to have bigger outreach with no hassle, so why not?

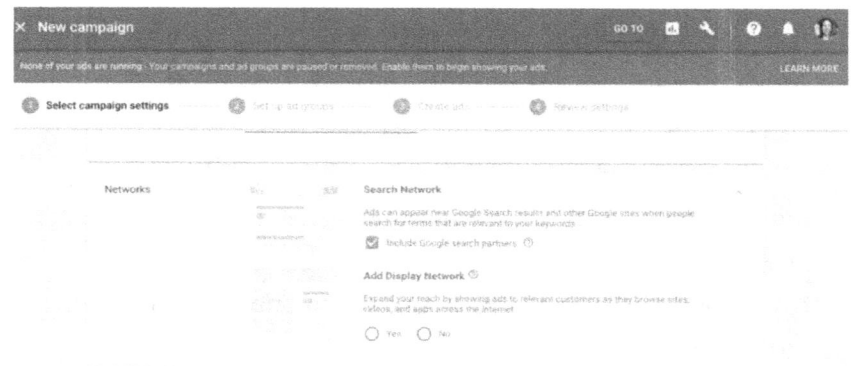

Creating a new campaign in the new interface of Google AdWords

Location and Languages

This section is crucial on the Campaign level. You can only target a specific geography on the campaign level. If you, for example, have a strict budget you would like to spend on a particular market only; then it is important that you create a separate campaign targeting only this location.

Don't select all countries and territories. Ever. This setting will spend your budget quickly and you will most likely end up with very bad results. If you are serious about your business, you must already know which countries and territories you would like to target.

Actually, Google allows you to be very specific here. If you choose the Advanced Search, you can select a Radius you would like to target. You can determine how big the radius should be (0-500mi/km).

Beware! In the old interface there is an option to select locations people are based in or searching for. This is also not recommended, as it expands your reach from people based in the U.S.A. to people from all over the world looking for information about the U.S.A., for example.

When it comes to language, you can choose the languages spoken in this location. If you prefer to target certain language – for example French speakers in the U.K.

Figure 2 location targeting by radius around a geo location

Budget

This is the daily maximum of spending you will allow Google to make on your campaigns. Beware that Google may still charge you more than your daily limit. It used to be up to 10% more, but since recently this is limitless. However the rule is that over 30 days your average daily cost will match what you have set up in your budget. This allows Google more flexibility, as there are times when people start searching for certain keywords a lot and there are times when it is very quiet.

Attention: If you click on Delivery method you will have two options – Standard or Accelerated. Make sure you are using Standard Delivery Method. Accelerated Delivery is a setting which tries to spend your budget as quickly as possible. Even if you have big funds, this setting will most likely leave you with some very expensive conversions and bad return on investment. You don't want that. You might be wondering, why is this setting there then? Well, I am not sure, but quite a few newbie advertisers have fallen into its trap.

Bidding Strategies

Google is implementing more and more bidding automation which is great but you must know what works best for your business goals before you choose a bidding automation. When you first create a campaign in the new interface you will be asked if you want to focus on clicks, conversions, conversion value and then choose if I want to bid manually or maximise conversions. What do they mean?

These are simplified names for ready bidding strategies which Google has for advertisers who are not sure what they are doing to guide them. Let's go through them and see what they mean.

Maximise conversions

This strategy is good if you don't have historical data, but bear in mind what you say then is: Google, please spend all my budget and get me the maximum amount of conversions you can, no matter on what cost. You can test this, but don't expect your conversions to be cheap. In cases when your budget is very limited and you would like to get any conversions, no matter what cost, you can go on and select this automation. Overall, not bad for beginners, but still not optimal.

Target ROAS

If I choose conversion value – this is a strategy which used to be called Target ROAS (target on return of advertising spend). So let's say I know every sign up I get is bringing $10 to my business. I would like to get a conversion on a cost less than 10$ so I have a positive return on ad spend. You can use the following formula to calculate your ROAS:

ROAS= total revenue/ad spend

The automated strategy will try to find conversions which give you good return on advertising spend. This can be useful if you already know your ROAS, but if you are completely new to advertising this might be just an assumption on how much you want to spend and what you expect as revenue.

Maximise Clicks

Only recommended if your goals are to build brand awareness Clicks do not equal conversions and usually you pay per click.

If your Google AdWords Account has a good history of a lot of conversions, you can try an automated strategy – no problem. Google will optimise on the past performance. If you don't, then I would stick to something less automated until you have enough data.

Manual CPC

Choose *Select a Bid Strategy Directly*. Then the least automated strategy is manual CPC(cost per click). This is the strategy which gives you the most control over spending, but it also is the highest maintenance one. It requires constant tweaking, adjusting and monitoring to make it work.

ECPC

If you select Manual CPC, you can also tick the box for enhanced CPC. This is a semi-automated strategy, which does not require any previous conversion history. ECPC looks for ad auctions which are more likely to lead to conversions and then raises your max CPC bid (after applying any bid adjustments you've set, if any) to compete harder for those clicks. If a click seems less likely to convert, AdWords will lower your bid. ECPC will try to keep your average CPC below the max CPC you set (including bid adjustments) but may exceed your max CPC for short periods of time.

Target CPA

CPA stands for cost per acquisition. The strategy tries to get you as many conversions as possible with your budget for a fixed cost per conversions, you set up.

This strategy has been developed into a beautiful machine learning powered technology by Google. Due to its poor performance few years ago, a lot of advertisers are still very snobby towards Target CPA and avoid it. It does perform beautifully over time, bringing expected volume on a flat cost per conversion. There is one problem. Machine learning must be fed with data and if your account has small or no conversion history, the automation will struggle.

Setting up the right Target CPA is a bit of an art itself, but also pretty logical. First of all you must have at least 30 conversions in the last 30 days before setting up Target CPA. If you have less than this, the campaign will need more time to learn, and it might end up not learning at all.

When you first set up Target CPA, it is just so tempting to choose the lowest possible cost per acquisition. This is the goal, right? Now, Google gets me these cheap conversions!

It does not work this way. If your CPA is too low, the campaign will simply not perform. Google will try to get you these cheap conversions, but since your account history does not provide it with information when and how to get them, it will not find many opportunities.

When you choose Target CPA as a bidding strategy you will have a recommended amount for a CPA coming as a suggestion. Take this suggestion. This is usually the realistic price you have been paying for a conversion the last 30 days. If you want to reduce this, you can do this gradually, leaving at least 2 weeks between changes to allow the campaign to learn. What works best is gradually lowering with maximum 10% on your CPA every two weeks or more.

Over time you will see what is the lowest possible CPA for your account without sacrificing the volume of conversions your business needs.

One big alert! Target CPA cannot function if your campaign is limited by budget. One of the reasons a lot of advertisers avoid it because when they set it up, they get a message the campaign has spent its daily budget the next day. Also, in the beginning, you will see a very big jump in cost per conversion, followed by a very low cost. This is the campaign learning – it is simply trying to find the sweet spot for you. Over the next 30 days, the cost per conversion will even out. At the end of the period, if you divide the amount spent by the number of conversions, you will get exactly the CPA you wanted.

It is really important that you don't make any adjustments on bids and keywords during this period. This will allow the algorithm to learn. What Target CPA does is taking complete control over your bids, changing them to bid more aggressively when historically data shows you are likely to get conversions. It will take into consideration any customer data which you provide – lists of emails of customers, remarketing lists of web visitors to bid higher when these people, or similar to them are searching for the keywords you bid on. (I will teach you how to set up these later when we talk about remarketing). It will rotate your ads so the best performing ones appear at the right time. It is a fairly sophisticated machine learning solution and is proven to beat a human advertiser bidding manually every single time.

The reason why a lot of people give up of this strategy so quickly is the clumsy initial learning period. It spends a lot in the beginning and it might look irrational first. Remember, the more conversion history you have in your account, the faster the CPA will learn and the better results you are going to get.

Target Search Page Location

This strategy as it comes from its name tries to place your ad on a certain position in the search results, no matter what it takes. Yes, no matter what it takes. I don't recommend it unless you are trying to please the ego of a client who desperately wants to search and see their ad first every time. It is expensive and might result in a lot of people clicking by mistake. Explain this to your client and if they are ready to pay premium for this position – let it be, but you are not responsible for the soaring cost per conversion.

In summary – Target CPA is great for advertisers who have a lot of conversions over the last 30 days and are okay with a higher spending to get a big volume of conversions in return.

Target Outranking Share

If you are in a war with a competitor and you are trying to win by showing your ad more, this strategy is for you. Same like Target Search Page Location – it is expensive and rarely necessary.

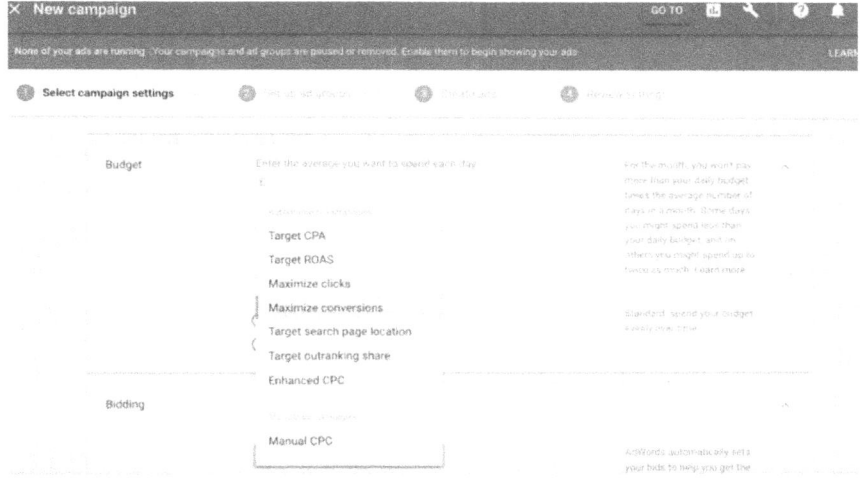

Figure 3 bidding strategies list - a lot of choices

Next step is setting up start and end date – pretty self-explanatory – you can schedule your campaign over certain time you would like to promote.

Dynamic Ads

Dynamic ads are ads which change their headline text according to what the user is searching for and automatically bid for keywords you have on your website. It is a bit of a tricky feature to set up for a beginner.

This type of ads were highly adopted by websites like eBay and Amazon which miraculously showed anything you search for in their ad, including a perpetual motion machine.

Old Dynamic ads were often leading to funny combinations.

To use it you can either allow Google to take over all the pages from your website which they have indexed and use them to create dynamic ads, or submit a page feed. A page feed is nothing but a spreadsheet you can upload in Google AdWords with two columns – page URL and Custom Label. Under page URL you must have all the pages you want Google to use for dynamic ads and under Label you can create custom labels for popular products based on their characteristics. For example, if you advertise hotels, each 4-star rated hotel can be labelled "FOUR_STAR; "POPULAR_DESTINATION"; and so on. You can download a free template from Google's support page.[2]

To upload the spreadsheet, go to the little wrench sign in the new interface, then select Business Data in the Setup column. Click the plus button and select Page Feed. Choose the file you have prepared with your URLs and Custom Labels. Then Apply.

You can then come back to the campaign you are setting up and choose Use URLs from my Page Feed only.

Audiences

---

[2] https://support.google.com/adwords/answer/7166527?co=ADWORDS.IsAWN Customer%3Dfalse&hl=en

We will cover audiences in much more detail when we talk about Display advertising and remarketing. Here you can choose lists of people who have visited your website, lists of emails of your current customers or subscribers, certain demographic groups (women between 25-35, for example), audiences similar to your lists or website visitors and other variations by interest and buying intent.

Remarketing Lists for Search (RLSA)

If you are using Target CPA bidding strategy, then adding audiences is really important. What it means is that the automated strategy will bid higher for people who have been already on your website and are searching for your product again, or similar to those people. Have you ever noticed how after you have been on a certain website, suddenly they start appearing on the top of your search results whenever you search the same product again?

This is called Remarketing Lists for Search, or RLSA. In the following chapters, I will explain how to create lists of website visitors and how to add lists of customers' emails to your Google AdWords Campaigns.

One very important note here. If you are adding any list to your search campaign, make sure you choose Observations, instead of Targeting below the Audience setting. If you choose Targeting this means your ads will appear only when someone who is on your list is searching for the keywords you are bidding on. This is a very limited audience, so your ads will not appear much. Observations allow your ads to appear when anyone is searching for your keywords. Then you can either make an adjustment to bid higher when someone from the list is searching, or if you use any automated bidding strategy it will automatically bid higher.

Extensions

Ever noticed how some ads appear very big and prominent on the search results? They have star review, a phone number, address and more text. This is all because of extensions. Google allows advertisers the same amount of ad copy, but if an ad is using extensions it is likely to get a better rank and show much more information.

Remember when we talked about the ad auction? Advertisers who bid high enough and have good quality score get a higher ad rank, but if they also use many extensions, then they are very likely to be on the top position.

In the new interface, you will be forced to add some extensions to your ads. If you skip them, Google will keep reminding you.

What types of extensions are there?

Sitelink extensions

Sitelink extensions are shortcuts to different relevant pages on your website. For example, if you are showing an ad about a university course, you can add several links to other related courses or the online application page. This increases the chance to match what the user was actually searching for, allowing some space for discovery.

You must have at least four sitelink extensions. Google will rotate all the ones you have to show the best-performing ones. In some cases, two sitelink extensions appear under the ad, in other cases four.

Callout Extensions

Callout extensions are short pieces of text – usually couple of words. There is no link related to them. They appear under the ad copy in a row. The callouts are just reminders of certain features your product or service has, for example, 24h support, Trusted, Recognized, Award-Winning, etc.

Call extensions

This is a phone number which appears in your ad. The phone number allows mobile users to directly call your business through the ad. In some cases Google might pick up the phone number associated with your business from Google Maps, if you are listed there. It is always better if you provide a phone number related to the business with an extension to make sure the right number appears in each location you advertise.

For example, you may have different offices around the world and your customer would prefer to talk to the one nearest to them. You can set up a calling extension for each of the campaigns you are running with a local phone number for this geographic location.

Message Extension

This is similar to the call extension but allows users to send a text message to the business. You can choose a different phone number for the message extension from the one you are using for the call extension. It will usually appear under your ad with a message balloon icon and text like: *Send us a text for more information.* This is suggested copy; you can easily modify it. When a user sends a text message they will get an automatic answer from the business with something like *I want to know more* or *How can we help you?*

Location Extension

This is usually the address of the business with opening hours and sometimes also phone number. As you can imagine this extension is connected with the listing of your business on Google Maps. The platform businesses use to claim their locations on Google Maps is called Google My Business(formerly Google Locations). To claim your location, you must create an account there and enter your address. Then Google will send a printed postcard to your address with an identification number. You must enter the number in Google My Business to verify that you are present at this location.

Once this is done, you will be able to see your location extension available in your Google AdWords account. If you have multiple locations, you can select the ones you would like to be shown in a certain ad group or campaign.

Review Extensions

Review extensions are now retired, so not much you can do about this. These were based on reviews you have received on online listings like Google Maps, Yelp or other reputable sources. You might still see star reviews related to certain ads, but these are automatically inserted from Google now, not something the advertiser can influence.

Structure Snippet Extension

This is just another row of text, added usually under the callout extensions. It is an opportunity to mention variations of a product you offer. You can choose from a dropdown menu – Amenities, Brands, Courses, Destinations, Models, Styles, Shows etc. Then you can list up to ten different variations. In an ad this would look like – Destinations: Morocco, Ibiza, Malta, Sardinia, Malaga. There are no links associated with the variations.

Promotion Extension

Promotion extensions look like a line under the ad copy with a price tag icon next to them. The promotion can be around an occasion like Christmas, Black Friday, etc. You can make a promotion with a monetary discount, per cent and also include "up to" type of discount. There is an option to add details like a promotional code, for example. The Promotion Extension can be scheduled and can have a separate URL to a special page just showing your promotional offer.

Price Extension

These are similar to promotion extension, but provide bigger visibility for a certain product or service. They will appear in little cards under the ad copy. They can be applied to products and services. You can choose units like per day, per night, per year, etc. Every item can have a separate URL leading to a page devoted to the product or product category. You can also schedule these extensions around a period when you want to push sales.

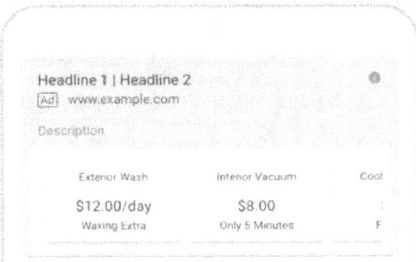

Figure 4 Price extension preview on a mobile device

App Extension

An app extension is a great way to urge people to install a mobile application you have created. You can choose between Android and IOS and then search for your app. If your app is available on both, you must create two extensions, because they will have different URLs. The extension can also be scheduled by dates and times of the day you would like it to appear.

Ad rotation

In the new interface this setting will appear under Advanced Settings and you will have *Optimise: Prefer best performing ads* pre-selected. Powered by Google's machine learning technology, the "Optimize" setting prioritises ads that are expected to perform better. You will see the options Optimise for Clicks and Rotate Indefinitely are no longer available. You can choose not to optimise, which will require you to check and measure success on a regular basis. I would recommend you to use the "Optimize" option to save yourself some time. If you are using an automated or "Smart bidding" strategy then it will apply rotation to optimise for conversions. For Manual CPC bidding the setting will focus on ads which are likely to attract clicks.

Same as Target CPA, some old generation advertisers are still snobby towards the ad optimisation automation. It used to be the case in the past, that if you add new ads in the campaign the Optimise setting will ignore them. This is no longer the case, trust me. The rotator immediately picks up new ads and if they are performing better within a few days you will see they have got more clicks than any of the old ad copies.

Campaign URL Options

You might not need to use this setting straight away. This is the place where you can bring Google AdWords data into your Customer Relationship Management system(CRM). CRMs are databases of customers data, where you can track what happens with a customer after they enter their contact details or make a purchase for example. Some widely used CRMs are Salesforce.com, Zoho, Swiftpage, SAP, Microsoft Dynamics, Oracle etc.

You are probably calling your customers on the phone after they have submitted an enquiry form, sending them emails, helping them with a product after they have completed a purchase. With a CRM system you can track these actions.

What is great is if you can bring the name of your campaign, the keyword or ad group which brought this person to you. This is why you can use a tracking template or custom parameter to bring this information in.

I will not go into the technicality on how to set up your CRM system to receive this data. This is different from product to product and you can confirm this with your provider.

What is a tracking template?

Have you noticed when you click on an ad the URL which you see is sometimes extremely long and complicated? If you look at it carefully, you will see something like:

https://www.example.com/online-course?utm_source=GoogleAdwords&utm_medium=search&utm_campaign=Employer%202018

You can easily cut all the words and signs after the question mark and you will still be able to load the same webpage. So why this long URL?

All the words after the question mark are part of a tracking template this advertiser is using to see who their ads are performing. UTM stands for Urchin Tracking Module. The utm is followed by an underscore and then the metric you are looking to import. Most often you will see utm_source, utm_campaign, utm_medium, utm_device and utm_keyword. These are standard fields. You can decide what you would like to import for each of these in. For you utm_campaign might be equal to something different than the actual campaigns names in Google AdWords.

If you set up tracking, you can send potential customers to specific landing page URLs that have extra information, like the keyword that triggered your ad or the type of device that the person who clicked your ad was using. When an ad is clicked, this information will be added to your final URL to create your landing page URL. A tracking template created at the ad group, campaign or account level applies to all of the ads in the corresponding ad group, campaign or account.

A tracking template might look like this:

{lpurl}&utm_source=GoogleAdwords&utm_medium=cpc&utm_term={keyword}&utm_campaign={_campaign}&utm_device={device}

What this means is, that anytime someone clicks an ad from this account, campaign or ad group, they will go to a URL with all this tracking information added after it. If they end up converting on this landing page, you will see in your CRM that their source is Google AdWords, they came in by CPC(cost per click) medium, they searched for something which included a specific keyword, their campaign was the one you specified in the campaign settings and also they used a mobile device to click on your ad.

What is a Custom parameter?

Custom parameters are an advanced type of tracking parameters which can be added at an account, campaign, ad group or ad level. You can add a custom parameter to your campaign and this will be picked up by your tracking template. For example, if your custom parameter is:

THE ULTIMATE ONLINE MARKETING GUIDE

Campaign URL options   Tracking template

Example: https://www.adwordstrackingtemplate.foo/?url={lpurl}&id=5

Custom parameters ⓘ

{_ campaign }   =   EU_Test_2018

{_ Name }   =   Value

{_ Name }   =   Value

and your tracking template says:

{lpurl}&utm_source=GoogleAdwords&utm_medium=cpc&utm_term={keyword}&utm_campaign={_campaign}&utm_device={device}

Then in my CRM I will see that the campaign through which this customer came to me is EU_Test_2018.

One alert here! If you use custom parameters on lower levels, i.e. you are tracking your ad performance, AdWords will always pick the parameter at the lowest level. So, your campaign level parameter will be ignored. This means the lower the level you create parameters, the more parameters you have to specify, so that you don't lose data.

In this example, if you still want to have the name of the campaign and the name of the ad which brought the conversion, you must set up both _campaign and _ad parameters at ad level.

I understand tracking templates and custom parameters might be a bit too much for a starter, but it is good that you understand what they stand for when looking at the results from a campaign. Wrong tracking might be the reason you see skewed results in your CRM and end up taking wrong decisions.

So far we covered the Campaign settings, Bidding Strategies and Ad Extensions. This is a very big chunk of information and you might want to go through them again. I have a few recorded videos which explain some of these concepts again, so you might want to watch these on my YouTube channel, Odolena Kostova:

https://www.youtube.com/channel/UCpMuj_zjeqmeJgtO1oKCLlQ

Ad groups

After you have set up your campaigns it is time to start building your ad groups. After going through all the settings in the previous chapter, you can click save and you are on the second stage – Ad Groups. Here is how it would look like in the new interface:

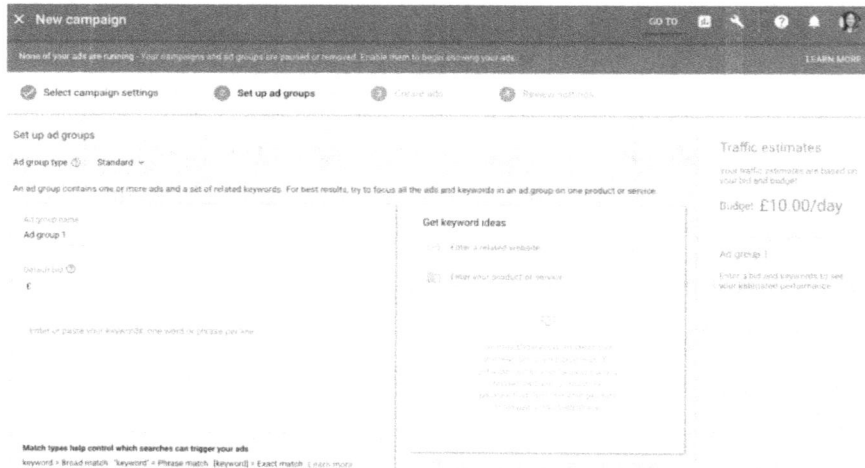

Why I love the new interface is because it is clean and emphasising on the simplicity of creating ads.

So what is an ad group?

Ad groups on the search network originated as a way to group your ads according to a theme. So in AdWords Search and ad group contains keyword/s and respective ads. Ad groups exist both on Search and Display advertising.

When creating search ad groups, you are looking for a theme of keywords to unite around a similar ad copy.

Remember when we talked about the importance of relevance between ad copy and keyword for a good quality score? This is where smart ad grouping comes in place. If I am looking to improve the quality scores of a client's account the first place I check is the number of keywords they have in an ad group and how related they are to the ad copy.

The recommendation in the early years of Google Ads was to have 10-15 keywords per ad group. However, since then the algorithms have changed and now are looking for a much closer relationship between an ad and a keyword. It is impossible to have an ad group with 10-15 keywords which are all really relevant to the ad copy you have.

The current best practice of Google is one keyword per ad group. The reason for this is that you can make sure that every keyword is very well related to the ads it is showing for. This sounds a lot, doesn't it?

Well, there are some ways to go around it and when we talk about keywords, I will explain exactly how you can use different keyword matches to cover many related terms.

On ad group level you must select a default bid for your ad group. This will automatically be applied to all the keywords in this ad group. If you want to change a keyword's bid you can do this manually.

4. GENERATING KEYWORDS

This is one of the most fun parts of creating a Google AdWords campaign. There are many tools you can use to generate great keywords and assess how they are likely to perform.

What exactly is a keyword?

A keyword can be a single word or a phrase. It can be even a very long phrase. Google matches this word or phrase to what someone is searching online. Depending on keyword match settings, advertisers can determine when and how often their ads to show and to which searches their ads can appear.

You can first start your research directly while creating a campaign. At ad group level (Figure 10) you can enter your website's URL and let Google suggest keywords for you based on your page. In the right-hand side, you will see various suggestions, which is already a good starting point for your keyword list. However, before adding them to the ad group, there are a few important things to know about keywords, which will save you a lot of efforts.

Keywords Matches

Not all keywords are born equal and first we must define how Google will choose on which searches to trigger your ad. There are four different ways you can choose your keywords to match search queries, which define how often you would like your ad to be shown. Showing your ad at irrelevant searches will damage your expected CTR(click-through ratio)and your Quality Score. Not to mention all the irrelevant clicks which have nothing to do with your business.

Let's imagine you are looking for a way to advertise a university course. Your main keyword is ***master's degree abroad***. These are three words and they can be searched in different order **degrees abroad masters**, users might other words in their search like: **how to apply for a master's degree abroad?** or break the phrase with other words like **degree abroad for a master's applicant.** Sometimes the original meaning can be completely lost by adding plurals and typos: ***masters sailing on Sunday how many degrees temperature aboard***.

You think it's too complicated a search? Once you see what people actually search for these days, you will be amazed. The level of complexity and variety of searches on Google is astonishing. Also, the increasing influence of voice search devices and apps like Siri, Cortana, Alexa, OK Google etc. is translating human speech into written text searches. These searches are longer and usually very specific, trying to get an immediate solution.

How to control your ads and make sure you appear in front of the prospective masters' students, instead of the sailing aficionados?

Very simple with keywords matches. Keyword matches control the way Google matches your keyword to the search query. Let's go through the options.

Broad Match

Dangerous territory. A broad match will allow your ad to be triggered by any search which contains any of the words in your keyword, OR their synonyms and plurals. This gives you zero control over the searches you appear for and expands your reach to thousands of people. You will reach a lot of people, but not many of them are likely to be happy with the result. Unless this is your brand or a really specific term, I would not recommend you to use any keywords in broad match.

Broad Match Modified

This match type is quite useful because it gives you a lot of reach but still helps you control the context. If your keyword consists of three words, broad match modified or BMM will allow your ads to appear on searches which contain all three of the words. They can be in any order, broken by other words.

All keyword matches will allow now plurals, abbreviations, shortenings and common typos to match the keywords. You no longer need to add these as separate keywords. If you see an account containing these variations, these are all now duplicates and should be paused. Having duplicate keywords in your account can result in awful quality scores and soaring costs. The new interface will give you the recommendation to pause all duplicates with one click. Make use of this recommendation.

Phrase Match

Phrase match is a type which can provide some double meanings of your word combination by fixing the order the words are shown in the search query. For example, a "hilton paris" will never trigger an ad on a "Paris Hilton" search query. The phrase match type will lock the word order of your keyword and not allow any other words to break in between the phrase. No "Hilton in Paris" – this will be a separate keyword. Additional words before and after the phrase keyword will be allowed. So **where is Hilton Paris located?** will trigger an ad. As with all keyword matches – typos, plurals and shortenings will be allowed.

Exact Match

Exact match is a way to disable any additional words to appear in the search query. No words will be allowed to appear before or after the keyword or break between the phrase. The words in the exact match keyword can since last summer appear in different order and include abbreviations, shortenings and plurals.

Negative Keywords

Every one of these match types can also act also as a negative keyword. Using negatives is a must when you are bidding on any type of keyword match except for exact, which prevents your ad from showing for all searches except for the actual keyword.

Negative keywords can be also broad, exact and phrase match. The difference is that the more searches a match allows when bidding on, the more searches it blocks when used as negative. I will illustrate this with an example. Imagine, you are working for a fashion e-commerce. You are bidding on the keyword *+plaited +skirts* in broad match modified. You would like to sell these skirts, but you don't want to attract clicks from people looking for let's say *pictures of girls in plaited skirts*. You decide to put the keyword *pictures of girls* in negative. However, now you risk blocking relevant searches like *buy plaited skirts for girls* or *online store* *plaited skirts pictures*. What you can do then is to put *pictures of girls* as a phrase match. In this case your ad will not be triggered by searches containing this precise combination of words in this order, i.e. phrase.

In other cases, your business name might be also a synonym or an abbreviation of something completely different. For example, in 2017 Nike put on the market snickers called Nike Kobe 11 Elite "Master of Innovation". In the same time, the number of universities advertised *master's degree in innovation*. Even now, a year later, if you make a Google search for Nike Master of Innovation, you will still get a number of prestigious business schools showing ads above the organic results of Nike. This is wasted money staring you in the face. It could have been prevented with a couple of clicks, by adding the [nike master of innovation] in your negatives as an exact match. Sorted.

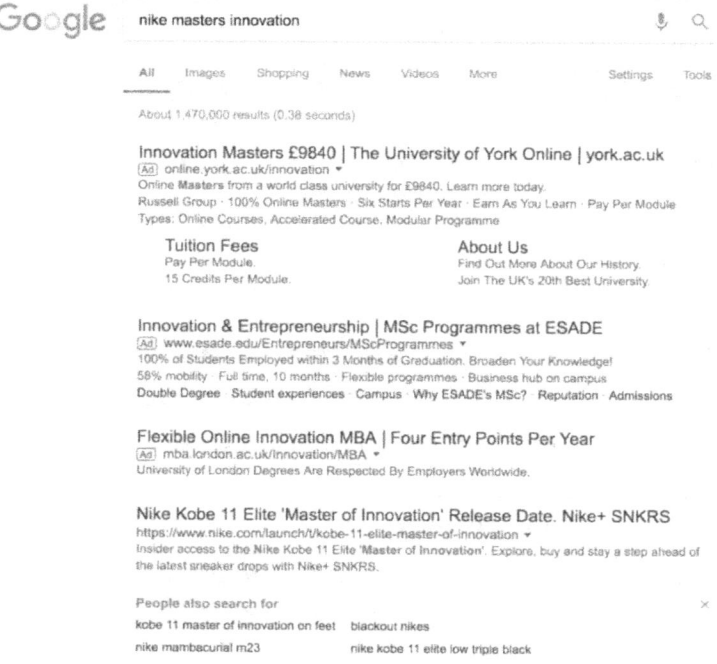

How to find negative keywords?

This is, of course, unique to your business and niche. One piece of advice - do not rely on the obvious. Users have unique ways of behaviour online. They might be using words which you cannot guess on your own. There are some great tools which can show you precisely what users who clicked on your ad actually typed in.

Search term report

This is the first place I would get to when I am assessing the performance of an account. To access the report in the new interface, go to Keywords, and then you have to choose Search terms. The other option Auction Insights, I will cover in the advertisement copy section. If you are using the old interface, you will have to follow the same pathway.

The Search Term report gives you precise information on how many clicks and impression every search term got. If you have conversion tracking installed, you will see also which search terms resulted in conversions(sales, sign-ups, opt-ins).

These are not the keywords you are bidding on, but the precise queries which people typed in and triggered the ad. To be in the report, a search term must have resulted in an impression (your ad appeared). You can see the average position on which your ad appeared and how much was your cost per click if there was a click.

If you click on the Columns icon in the new interface(Columns, then Modify Columns in the old one), you can select different metrics to see. You can add the keyword which triggered the ad. You will see a column, showing whether this search term is the same as a keyword you already bid on or have added to negatives. If you are bidding on it it will show with a green tick box saying "added", if it is already a negative you will see a red cross and "excluded". If you see "none" it means that this search term is new – it is a mix of your keyword combined with other words.

In the new interface only, you will see by default the first column as Match Type. This will show you how closely the search term matches your keyword – whether it is exact, phrase or a close variation. This can help you find ideas for new keywords or old keywords you could be used with a different match type.

For example, if you see that 90% of your conversions come from "purple roses" in exact match and you have this as a broad keyword, you might consider having it as exact, too. In this way you can bid higher when someone is using an exact match of your keyword and a bit less when it is a more complex variation.

In the past advertisers solved the lack of this information making a separate campaign for the same keywords in broad, phrase and exact. In this case they add all the keywords from the exact campaign as negatives in the broad and the phrase. The reason for this is because the broad and phrase campaigns will take away traffic from the exact one and you will never know what the impact of your exact match keywords. Now since Google AdWords added the match type in the search term report such granular approach is not necessary.

The Overview Report

Quite handy, Google added a small table in the new interface under Overview – usually the home page of your account where you can see if your ad appeared for any new searches. There might be a new trend - a reality show or hit song which triggers your ad just by the unfortunate combination of words. I keep on discovering new searches which have nothing to do with my product but still trigger my ads. You can immediately exclude these searches by adding the new terms ad negative keywords.

Also this can give you some ideas about new topics people are searching for. People's interests and market trends change all the time. If you are using some broader keywords, you can easily spot new search terms people use and jump on trends as they go.

Trust me, there is nothing better than catching a trend earlier. I have realised with time that the majority of businesses do not research trends and searches consistently and therefore you easily can find yourself to be the first one in a new market. The more you can escape from what everyone else in your market is doing, the better chance you have to have a breakthrough. In the following chapters I will show you some tools which will help you see trends early on, spot consistent behaviour and identify new keywords.

How to select great keywords?

Keywords are the backbone of your account. When you first start, you must do some research. Google AdWords has one of the best search trends tool available no matter if you do paid advertising or not. The Keyword Tool can show numbers of searches per month for different words or phrases. In this way you get to learn what are the popular search terms and get ideas for your keywords.

In the new interface you can navigate to the Keyword Tool by clicking on the wrench icon and selecting Keyword Planner in the Planning column.

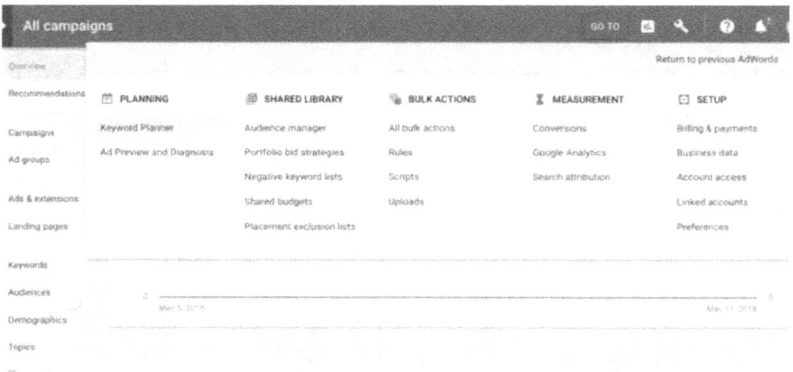

What follows is a page where you can search for a phrase to start getting ideas and data. Let's say, you are looking to create an account for an online textbook store. You search for a generic term like *buy used textbooks online* and then get search trends for a period you select. You can choose to see results for a specific geographic location, language and select whether you would like to see data from Google only, or also include its search partners. You get a graph like this:

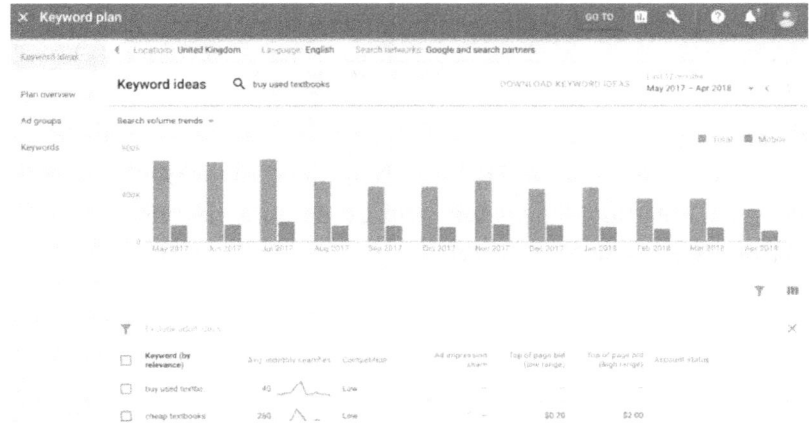

What is great is that under the graph you have a whole list of other keywords which could be relevant for you and their search trends. The first column gives you average keyword searches per month. You must aim for keywords which do get a lot of searches. Low volume keywords might be cheaper, but there is a reason why. Usually they have a slim chance of getting impressions or even less clicks and just take space in your account.

The next metric which is important is the level of competition. If you see a keyword has high competition, this does not mean you should ignore it. It means that probably it is a perfect keyword, since everyone wants to appear on it. However, it might be expensive, so you must be ready to bid higher and to work more on your ad content and landing page to make sure the effort is worth it.

Another metric you get to see is the Search Impression Share. Search Impression share is from the times when this search term is searched how many times was your ad triggered. You will only get this data, if you have ad history in your account and if the search term you are checking has triggered any of your ads.

Then you will see the top of the page and first page bid estimations, which will give you an idea of the conversion cost for you. If you know your average conversion rate there is a simple way to estimate how much your conversion will cost.

For example, if my conversion rate is 10% and the average CPC for this search term is £5, then for 100 clicks I will pay £500. I know that just 10 of these clicks will end up as conversions, so my cost per conversion will be £500/10 = £50.

If I know that each of these conversions is worth £1000 for my business, based on the formula we used in the Auction chapter, then it is obvious that this could be a good keyword for me. I can try to increase my conversion rate by improving my landing page and adding relevant negative keywords and may achieve a cheaper cost per conversion.

In the last column, called Account Status, you will see if this keyword is in your account already, if it is negative, or if you have added it to a plan.

Once you spot a good keyword, you can add it with just a click to a plan. Simply tick the box next to the keyword and select ad to plan. Your plan can contain different ad groups based on a common theme. You can choose if you want the keyword as negative and in what match.

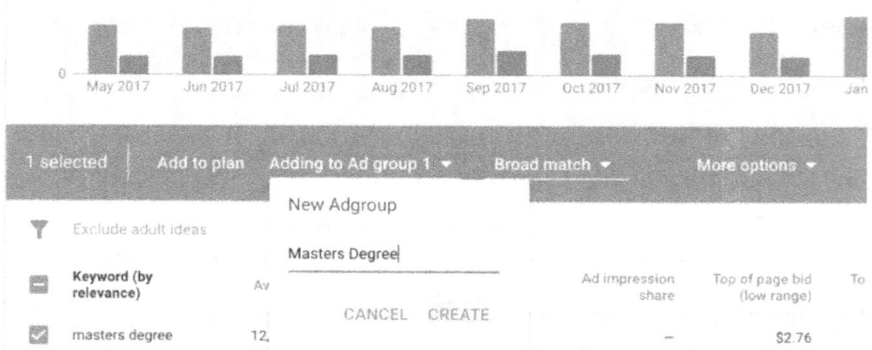

At the right side of the stats you can review your plan and get estimated clicks, impressions, conversions — all calculated for you. You can estimate this on ad group or keyword level. I do not always take this estimation as an ultimate truth, as it is precisely an estimation based on the account history. It does not take into consideration any negative keywords you already have and the picture might be a little bit exaggerated.

The best way is to add the keyword you are interested in your account and see the results live. As long as you monitor it carefully, you are not risking. You can add the keywords from the Keyword Planner to your account directly, but you must create a new campaign. If you want to add them to an existing one, you can download the list and the estimations in a spreadsheet and upload them in your campaigns.

Keyword Research

There are multiple tools you could use besides the Keyword Planner. One of the easiest ones is Google search, itself. Just put the keyword you would like to research and see the search suggestions generated by Google. These are all the other most often searched queries related to the keyword.

Also after you hit Enter you will get a group of search suggestions at the bottom of the results. These are usually longer phrases which are great if you want to get to specific audience, like in the example of the used textbooks keyword – medical students.

Google Trends

Another great way to see interest in certain areas over time is Google Trends. It is not really a keyword generation tool, as it shows more general audience behaviours over time. You can estimate relationships between different search terms and see popular topics in certain regions. To access the global Google Trends go to https://trends.google.com/ If you prefer you can check the Trends version for your country.

If I go to the U.K. version of the website https://trends.google.co.uk/trends/ I first see the top events happening in the country at the moment. I just love this screenshot from Google Trends U.K. which I did in May 2018:

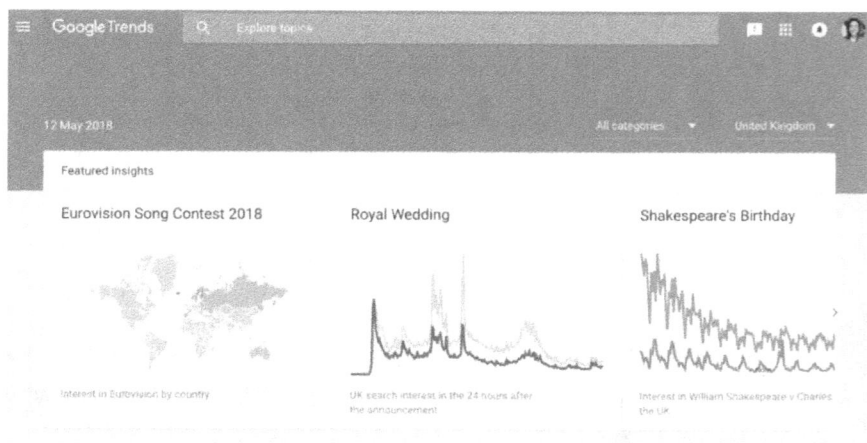

Scrolling down there is a selection of the most read news articles and in this day, popular sports events, movies or TV shows.

The best part is the Explore Topics search field. If we do search for a generic term like *vodka*, we get typically several suggestions:

Vodka as a Search Term, which is the broadest approach, if you really want to see all the searches simply containing this word without any context.

Vodka as an Alcoholic Beverage, which will take out any searches which do not refer to vodka in this context, like movie and book titles, for example.

Vodka as in Absolut Vodka topic. This will filter only the interest in this specific brand of vodka. Further down you will see Smirnoff, which is a popular brand, but it does not contain the exact search term vodka.

Let's choose just vodka as a search term to get the most information. If we choose a twelve months' time frame and worldwide location we will see a peak in the searches, just before the New Year's Eve celebration.

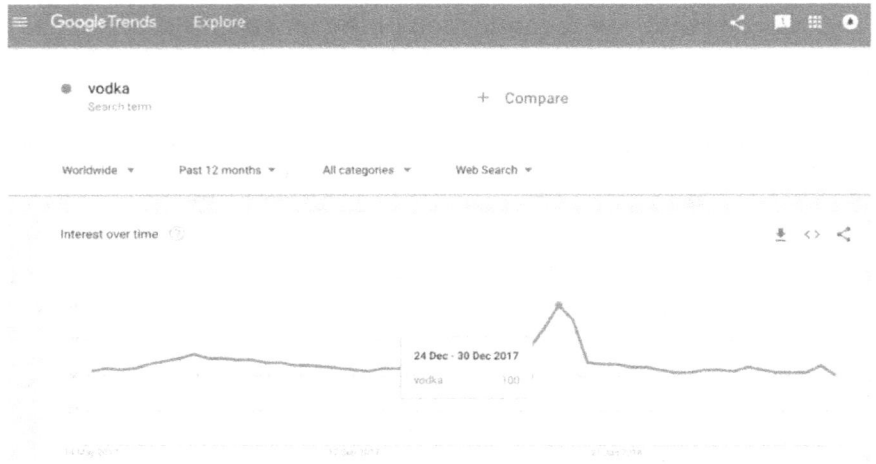

If we expand the timeframe to 5 years we will see this happening periodically in more or less the same day every year. Pretty much like a pulse:

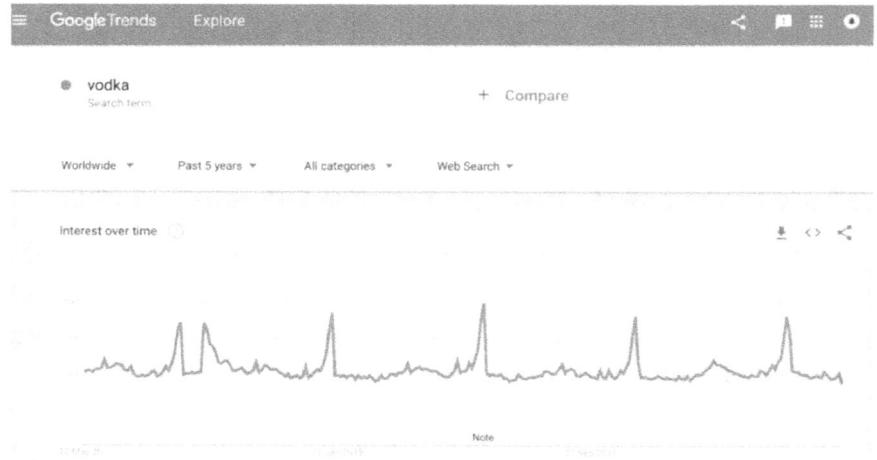

What is great is that you can compare this to another term and see the correlation in time. If compare vodka and hangover over the last 5 years we will see that these are not surprisingly correlated. Hangover searches always increase after New Year's

Eve, when people are looking for cures. The big spike in 2013 is most likely the release of the Hungover movie. Other than that the trend is clear:

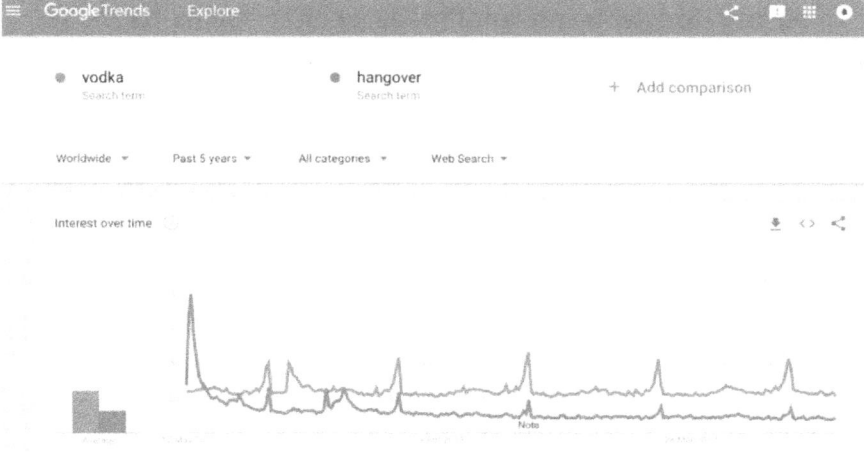

If you scroll down you can see the interest per region for both terms which you are comparing. What I find great is the most popular searches containing this word. The hangover search actually includes a lot of popular topics which take the term in different context like a song's name, a movie or popular meme.

You can choose whether you would like to see the rising or top queries. This can help you identify behaviour trends; what people are interested in right now and in general over time.

I find the Google Trends tool great when it comes to analysing why certain campaigns go quiet over time. Also, how it works at the moment is really a gold mine for content creators. If you are looking for topics for your blog there is no better source of ideas.

SEMrush

This is one of the best research solutions for marketers today (https://www.semrush.com/). This is a website which allows you to investigate a keyword, a domain or URL and get more or less full picture of how they rank on Google, organically and with paid advertising, which keywords they bid on, who else bids on these keywords.

If you do a search for *used textbooks* you will get estimated volume of searches and number of results. Then you get average CPC bid and level of competition. There is a useful table of what the CPC distribution is in several of the main global markets like U.S.A., U.K., India, Australia, Germany and Canada.

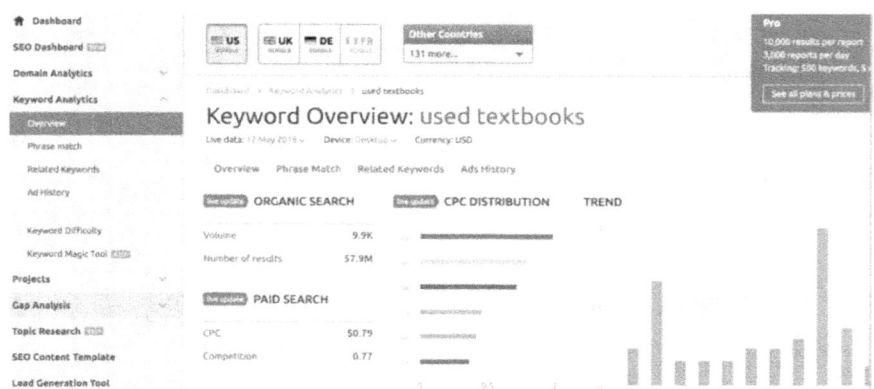

Then you get a list of search terms you will appear for if you use the keyword in phrase match on Google AdWords with search volume and CPC estimation. Next, you have a list of related keywords with their estimated monthly volume and CPC.

What I love about SEMrush is the list of top organic search results ranking on this keyword and the top advertisers. You will get some of these if you conduct a simple Google search, but this is limited to your location. If I want to find out which the top-ranked organic results in Germany are I must be searching in this country. The same is valid for top advertisers. With Google AdWords it is possible to see a preview of the auction in a different country, but you will only get a few of the top results. In SEMrush you will get eight top ads on Google AdWords for this search term in any of the main global markets.

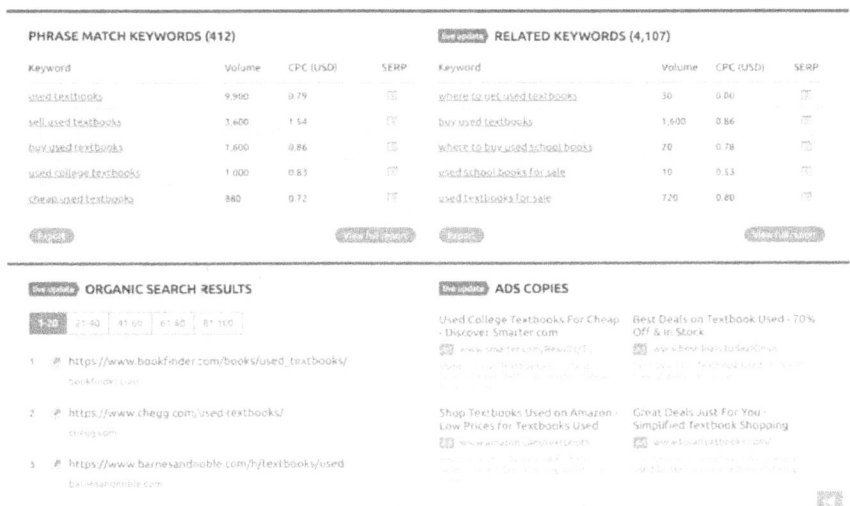

The problem with SEMrush is that only a small portion of it is available for free. For a longer list of keywords, extra reports and more searches, you have to pay. Monthly fees start from $99, but it is an investment which can help you a lot.

SmiliarWeb

This is the ultimate competitor research tool (https://www.similarweb.com/). Remember all those top advertisers you saw in SEMrush? Well, if you enter their domain in SimilarWeb you will find out what other keywords they bid on. Let's take bookbyre.com for example.

When I entered the site in the tool, I get some information about the company – how old it is, where it is based, how it ranks globally, on its leading country level and in its main category. From this analysis we can see that bookbyte.com is not very highly ranked in the U.S. which is its leading country and also in its Book and Literature category.

Then we get some top-level analytics about their website like traffic in the last 6 months, average visit duration, pages visited on average in one session.

My favourite part is the traffic split. Here we can see how websites like this one get their traffic – which websites link to them, do they pay for any ads. For Bookbyte.com we can see that the main chunk of traffic comes from search engines and almost 20% of it comes from search engine ads. You will see the top 5 keywords they pay for and the top 5 keywords they rank most organically.

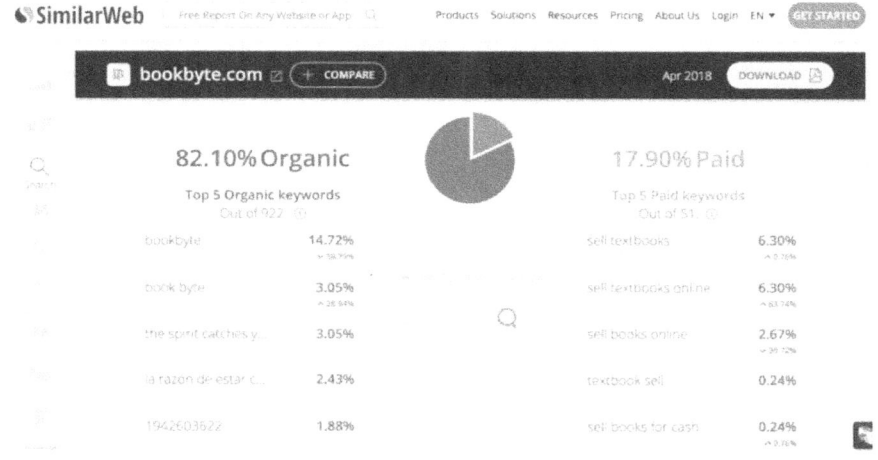

Further down you can see if they use any display advertising and where normally their ads are shown. You also have a list of similar websites and competitors you can research in the same way.

These are some of the main ways you can research keywords, competitors and behaviour trends online. This is really the most important part of your paid search marketing. Once you get a good list of keywords and relevant negative ones, you must test them in a live campaign.

Note that if you are using an automated strategy like Target CPA, you might not need many negative keywords as the campaign learns which searches are less relevant and not likely to get a conversion. It will bid very low for them so that your ad will have no chance to appear. You can test over time by leaving the automation take more and more decisions, but in the beginning start with a decent list of negative keywords and keep monitoring your Search Term report to spot odd ones.

5. CREATING ADS

This is the last stage before setting your first campaign live. Writing ad copy is actually much easier, than a lot of people think.

The only challenge is to get the most interesting and important part of your message in less than 40 characters. A typical Google text ad consists of

Headline 1 (30 characters with spaces)

Headline 2 (30 characters with spaces)

Description (80 characters with spaces)

Display URL (two paths – 15 characters each)

Final URL(no limit)

I have seen accounts with way too complex ads where obviously they tried to use every character to the maximum. This is not your goal.

What is the essential goal of an ad?

An ad has very limited space. The ad copy is really just a listing and there is no need or space to write a whole sentence. A successful ad must only focus on the absolute core of your value proposition. Most important, it must contain the keywords you are bidding on in this ad group, so that you get a good quality score.

The ad copywriting with so few characters is an art form in itself. You must use imagination and put yourself in the shoes of a prospective client. People who are searching on Google are not in the same mental state as when reading a blog article or an e-book. They are scanning for information. With the time we have all developed a hypersensitivity to weed out irrelevant stuff and immediately discover the most relevant information. Therefore, the closer you get to your keyword in the first headline, the bigger chance you get, first, to be selected by Google to show in the top results and second, to be selected by the user to click on your ad. As you can imagine, every time your ad is clicked this is a rare opportunity.

If your ad shows a lot but is not getting clicks your CTR(click-through ratio) drops down and this is a signal for Google, that people do not find your listing interesting and relevant to their searches. Google is aiming for making the search process as easy and simple as possible. Intuitive algorithms like Humming Bird, which was released in 2014, can "sense" the context of the search and show synonyms, close variations, images when it comes to the organic results. Google is even stricter with advertisers, because they know if the user does not find what exactly they are looking for in a matter of seconds they get frustrated. It is a mutual process, where people trust Google and keep using its search engine and advertisers keep coming to Google because this is where their customers are.

To help Google meet its goal, you must become their ally. Instead of trying to cheat the system, you must work in unison. In the past advertisers were able to push scam and bad quality ads to the top of the results, just by paying more. This led to users losing trust and avoiding ad clicking or Google. Ten years ago it was much more likely that you use a mix of Mozilla, Internet Explorer and Google. Since then all efforts were to make the ads as relevant as the organic search results. Today 90% of the search traffic is on Google.

Your Headline

In early 2017, Google replaced the existing text ad format with the Expanded Text Ads. This is when the ads on the right side of the search disappeared. Now there are 3-4 placements on the top of the search results and 1-2 at the bottom. Your chance of getting a click drops dramatically if your ad shows bellow position 3. This means more competition not only on price but mainly on quality.

The old text ads consisted of a single headline and a long description. Now Google replaced this format with two headlines, giving much more opportunity to shine with two bold messages.

Some rules you must be aware of:

- No exclamation marks in the titles
- No BLOCK CAPITAL words
- No other brand names

It is a common best practice that you capitalise all the words in your headlines to get more clicks. You might be worried about the grammatical correctness? Since all advertisers are doing it, having your ads without capitalisation might make it less attractive. It is a small detail which can be done or not done.

When it comes to the message, I usually follow a very simple formula:

Headline 1 = my main keyword

Headline 2 = Call to action

Be aware that Google will pick up if you provide any synonyms or relevant context to your keyword. For example, if my keyword is *women high-heeled shoes*, I can post the following ad:

Headline 1: Women's High-Heeled Shoes

Headline 2: Shop All Sizes. Real Leather

The words shoes, high-heeled, sizes, leather are all connected and give a context to the ad. It tells Google that it is intended for someone looking to buy. It gives extra context by identifying colour, material and size which is something likely to be important for a buyer.

The description part of the ad is great if you have any additional things to say like promotions, specific attributes to the product. In our shoe example, I would add:

Shop Our Hot Styles Added Weekly – Simple Browsing for Busy Fashionistas!

Exclamation marks are allowed in the description. You can also include important facts like time required, upcoming sale, 24-hour support, etc. The description is a good opportunity to mention your keyword again, but it is not a must. Try not to overstuff your ad with the keyword. Google awards ads which provide as much relevant and important to the customer information as possible. Using synonyms of the keyword and characteristics which provide the right context helps Google determine who this ad is for.

The last part of a successful ad is the URL to which you are leading the customers after they click on the ad. This URL is also known as Landing Page. There is a Display URL which consists of two "pathways" from 15 characters. This is not a real URL, but just a shortening of the original URL, which you create. It looks like this:

Example.com/pathway1/pathway2

You do not have to fill out both pathways if you do not have a reason. Normally the URL of your actual landing page will be quite long for it to fit under the ad. This is why Google gives you a chance to have a shortening of your choice. This is a great chance to stick your keyword in again and also to prepare the user for the landing page you will be taking them to if they were to click the ad. For example:

Example.com/shoes/red-heels

The final URL is the address of the landing page you have prepared for your ad. This user will not be see this. They will only see the domain of your website and the two pathways if you have filled them out.

Taking your ad copy to the next level

There is one way to find out what works to make sure your ads perform in the best ways possible – by testing. Google has now made it easier than ever before to test copy,

Dynamic ads

I briefly touched upon the Dynamic Ads when we were going through the campaign settings. To remind you, these ads adjust themselves to the search query of the users. They adjust not only the ad copy of the ad but also the landing page, sending the user to the page which is closest to what they are trying to find out on Google.

Plus of these ads is that they can really react to search queries and show the most relevant part of the website to the user. Some of the minuses are what you have no control over the ad copy. I have seen Google showing Dynamic Ads recommendations with ad copy which shows a different product from what I am offering. Far away from the example of "Perpetual Motion Machines", I showed in the previous chapter, Google still includes terms which do not match what I am offering. The second problem is that the landing pages they choose are not often the ones I want my prospects to go to. For example, the ad serving system selects pages which do not have a sign-up form, so the traffic cannot be captured. Many businesses have their converting tool(a sign-up form or a subscription) only on a few pages of their websites.

To summarise Dynamic ads are great, they improve the user experience and the relevance of your ads. However they are suitable for a business which offers a big variety of products and a website which can convert on every single page.

Ad rotation

As I mentioned Ad Rotation is one of the key campaign settings. You have the simple choice between optimising for best performing ads and rotating the ads evenly. Optimising is always recommended, regardless of your other settings. You will see some of the ads you want to show do not perform that well and it is OK.

We as business owners tend to take decisions on what we think our customers would like. Some features of your product you think are very appealing might have little meaning to the customer. Using optimisation for best performing ads and a variety of different ad copy in every ad group, helps you eliminate the assumption moments. Google will show only the ads which have the best chance of getting a click and creating value for your business.

Keyword Insertion, Countdowns and Ad Customizers

If Dynamic ads do not seem to be a good option for you, then you can make just part of your ad dynamic. Keyword insertion allows you to bring the exact search query in your ad's headline. Let's say you are selling a shoe in many colour variations. Instead of writing an ad for every colour, you can simply allow Google to insert the colour a user is looking for in the headline of your ad. When the query is too long, you can select a generic word to appear in your ad's headline instead.

A keyword insertion ad will look something like this:

{Luxury Shoes} for women

Order online now

Luxury women's shoes by UK's top designers. Online offer with free delivery.

The word in the curly brackets is the one which will appear if the search query is too long to fit in the headline. When a user searches for "party shoes" your ad will automatically turn into:

Party Shoes for women

Order online now

Luxury women's shoes by UK's top designers. Online offer with free delivery.

You can also include countdowns to a specific date. Let's say you have a limited offer by the end of the month. You can create a countdown to show the days left till the end of the sale dynamically in your ad every day.

Another option is an ad customizer. This gives you more control over what will show in the ad than a keyword insertion. If you offer several different products with varying availability in your stores, you can upload a simple feed(an Excel file) with this data into Google. When you build your ad, you can enter the location of the store as a customizer. In this way users will see only the closest to their location. All countdowns, customizers and keyword insertions work with curly brackets. For the first two, you need to upload an Excel file with your product, location or deadline feed before you start.

Auto-Applied Ad Suggestions

Google will periodically suggest ideas about new ad copy as a recommendation. These are based on current ad copy, extensions and landing page content. Consider applying these suggestions. They are a combination of your best-performing ad copy. You can always track how they perform versus your original ads and tweak them to fit your goals.

Responsive Ads for Search

The latest piece of Google Search's ad format evolution is the RSA (Responsive Ads for Search)[3]. They consist of three headlines and two descriptions. As you can imagine this is a huge piece of real estate on the Search results page. To create a responsive ad, the advertiser must provide 3-15 variations of the headlines and 2-4 variations of the descriptions. These will be automatically rotated and combined by the ad-serving system to find out the best performing combination.

It is possible to "pin" some of the Headlines (up to 2) to make sure they always appear as a first, second or third headline. However, the more restrictions you put on the campaign, the less value you can get out of the automated ad-serving. The pinning takes away the whole purpose of having a machine learning powered creative rotation.

For many advertisers, this is a challenge – there is no control over the appearance of the ad. Google is assuring that the algorithm will avoid redundant text side-by-side, but there is no way to really prove

---

[3] While writing this book RSA were still in Beta version, but Google had announced launching them for all advertisers in the fall of 2018.

it. Advertisers cannot see in which form their ads have appeared and must trust the machine learning to choose the best combination.

6. LANDING PAGES (BONUS)

Landing pages deserve to be in a separate topic, even though they are created outside the advertising platform of Google AdWords. The success of your ad, campaign and whole online presence depends highly on the pages to which you are sending traffic to.

I have seen numerous businesses which do not grasp the importance of their landing pages. No matter how beautiful your creative is, no matter how carefully you have selected your keywords, written your ad copy, specified your settings, you will not be successful if your landing page is bad. Period.

A landing page must be a designated page, not a generic homepage or a broad category on your website. It must be ideally dedicated to the precise predict you are advertising with your ad or keyword. You can have a Final URL on ad level or keyword level. If you are using a keyword level URL, your page must be as close as possible to the keyword you are bidding on.

When directing traffic to a landing page you must make it really clear and easy for the user to see what action you would like them to complete – fill out a form, subscribe, make a purchase, watch a video, etc. There must be no distractions like other links to content pages on your website or even worse to someone else's website. Remember, you have worked so hard to get this click and you have paid already for this user to come to the page, Now you must get a conversion.

When it comes to creating a great landing page, there are several musts which Google requires, simply so that you are not penalised straight away.

- Navigability. Your landing page must provide an opportunity to navigate to the main website. This can be done by clicking on your logo, as you are trying to clean any links which can distract the user from the action you want them to complete. However, Google also wants you to give a chance to the user to learn a bit more about you.
- Spiderability. This is purely technical part of building a landing page.
- No pop-ups. The days of pop-ups are gone, you mus

This is the technical part, but there is so much more to a successful landing page. Once you have the absolute minimum covered, which you will if you are not doing anything radically illegal online, you must focus on your strategy.

A successful landing page looks usually simple, but is not so easy to make. It takes some testing and research before you start getting great results.

One of the best ways of brainstorming good landing page is by checking out what your competitors are doing. I know your goal is to dominate, not to compete, but you can get some great ideas which are already working.

Step 1. Simply do a Google search for the keywords you are planning on bidding on and see which are the top results. You can also get this information from SEMRush which we talked about already.

What is a lead?

I know some of you are familiar with this term, but just to make sure it is clear for everybody. A lead is an email, phone, address, whatever contact information of a person who is interested in your business. A lead is a sale in the potential. Depending on how you approach leads after they show interest in your product whether you will get a sale or not. It can be by a call, a text, an email, direct mail, remarketing ad, social media message, in person visit or all combined. Whether you get a sale or not, depends 90% on your follow up efforts.

In this book, we will focus on two aspects of the lead generation — getting a lead and following up with retargeting or remarketing ads. I briefly wrote about remarketing with search, which is just a small portion of what you can do. I will go in much more detail about the remarketing campaigns you can set up with Facebook and Google Display ads.

A Lead Magnet

Step 2. Then see what your competitors have on offer — is it a free report, a book, a video, how do they convert their traffic. This is called the lead magnet — a piece of information which you exchange for their contact details. I have seen so many businesses completely ignoring this element.

You cannot apply any paid online campaign if your website cannot generate leads. I repeat. Your money and efforts on Google AdWords, Facebook or any other platform will be a complete waste if you don't have a landing page which converts cold traffic in leads.

A landing page must offer something of great value to the customer. In fact such great value, that they are ready to give their contact details to have it. A successful lead magnet has the following characteristics:

- It must be tightly related to what you are selling and what problem your customers are trying to solve.
- It must be easy to consume – short and sweet
- It must give some insightful information, some golden nuggets which they would have never expected for free

How to come up with a great lead magnet?

By doing research on your competitors and the whole industry. I like checking magazines, recent articles, publications, Twitter to inform myself about what is happening in the world of digital marketing. Also, I have a blog and active social media which give me an immediate response to what problems people are trying to solve. A successful social media post is not to be ignored. If something is getting attention, it is for a reason.

Create your lead magnet

Try getting some professional help when creating a lead magnet – might be from a freelancer or if you have your own designer, even better. There are some great places you can get designer support very cheap.

- Fiverr
- Freelancer
- F65

Just make sure the free item you are offering has good value. If it is a video, make sure it is well shot, with good sound and quality. If it is an e-book, make sure it has a well-designed cover and is proof-read.

You can even hire a ghostwriter to help you if writing is not your strength. A ghost-writer is someone who you can send voice recordings of your book and they can write it down in a professional manner for you. This might be more expensive, but if you have the money, go for it – you will save a lot of time and the risk of giving up.

Landing page layout

- A simple layout with fewer distractions is key. Some of the main elements of a good page are:
- Big promise, very specific title of a product which solves a common problem
- Big call to action button which makes it clear what is about to follow – sign up, download a PDF, join a webinar, get access to software, etc.
- A catchy image or even better a video of you explaining what value prospects are going to get if they opt in the free lead magnet. This creates a connection with the user and increases the chances of conversion.
- A few bullet points emphasising the main features of the product.

The Thank You page is the webpage where you redirect people after they have completed a conversion. It usually contains a thank you message and some further information.

However, I think the best part of it is that it allows you to introduce a paid product there. This is called an upsell. The reason why the Thank You page is the best place to introduce a sale is that users are already curious, they are in the mood of following your instructions. It is much harder to get them back if they are no longer on your website. The more time you allow from getting the lead magnet until you offer a paid product, the less likely you are going to get a sale.

What is a sales funnel?

A lot of marketers nowadays design their websites to make, what they call a funnel. A funnel is stages of offers to users, depending on their level of interest.

For example, you offer your free lead magnet to as many people as possible, trying to convert them. Then you offer them an upsell immediately after they become a lead. If they go for the upsell, then later they offer another product. At every level of the sales funnel a more advanced and expensive product is offered.

Why do you need a funnel type of website?

Well, it is proven to be working. A lot of websites are getting a big amount of traffic, but it does not convert into sales. The reason is that first, they don't capture any leads, second, they don't offer an opportunity to buy at the right time.

An average e-commerce would have several product sections with different categories of products. You will see the expensive ones and the cheap ones at the same place. People compare the offers and choose the cheaper option. The reason is that there is no value building. What would be the difference between a book about gardening and the full video course about successful gardening? Well of course, if you created them you know how much more information you have added in the course and therefore it is priced $100 more expensive than the book. However in the eyes of the average visitor this is not so obvious. Why bothering with a video course, since I probably would get the same information by getting the book for $10.

If you, however, present your products gradually one by one, creating a "value ladder" it is much more likely that someone who started with the cheapest product converts to a more premium offer.

First, you reduce the users' time and hesitations, by focusing on a single offer at a time.

Second, it becomes easier for them to see the increase in value at every stage of the ladder.

You gradually introduce the material and educate your audience. Otherwise, you are likely to introduce too advanced material to someone who is not ready to cope with it. They are not likely to understand or find much use from your product.

How to make a website with a funnel sales?

An online sales funnel can be created with some ready software – there are many options available on the market. However, they are pricey and you depend on the settings and templates which are pre-done for you. Since they are becoming very popular you see the same templates over and over again.

The best way is to get a website designed and customised for yourself.

The benefits are not only the cost saving but also your ability to have full control over the website. You can change the design, customise it to your needs and niche. A funnel type of website which is created with a popular template is so easy to recognise that you are unable to differentiate yourself from the competitors.

Busting myths about hiring a developer:

- It's expensive and unaffordable for a small start-up or a one-man firm.

Using a developer's help will eventually be less expensive than reoccurring monthly payments for a platform. (The most popular one, ClickFunnels is £230 per month!). If you hire a developer, you will have a higher up-front fee, but it will save you a lot in the long run.

- You cannot make easy "drag and drop" changes whenever you like.

Yes, with a ready drag and drop software you can make changes yourself, but think about how much time you are going to spend doing this. Working even with ready website created from WordPress still requires a lot of skills. Most businesses usually get to learn just how to post blog articles. For any other major change they ask for support. With a ready sales or e-commerce platform you are very limited to the changes you can make. This is why all websites look the same.

On top of being cheaper in the long run, much more flexible and unique, a professionally developed website is more secure. Google has now announced that they take preference for websites which have SSL and they appear higher in the organic results. These are the website which starts with https:// instead of http://

These types of websites keep secure sensitive information like credit cards and payment methods. A user will be warned by Google's browser when landing on a lead form page without SSL:

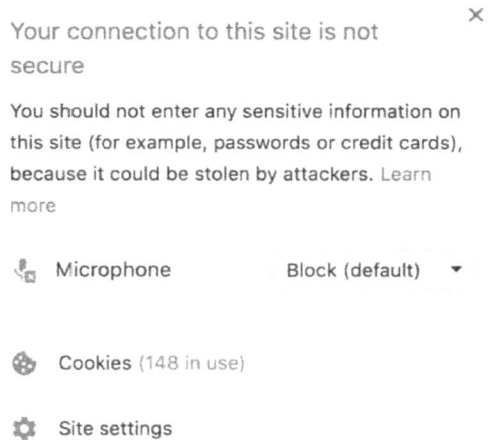

You don't want people to see this message on a page where they have to enter personal information like email, password or payment details. You also do not want your website to be downgraded in the organic results of Google because of the lack of SSL.

If you are interested in getting a customised professional funnel type of website, you can contact me on the form below. I work with a network of professional developers who created my website as a sales funnel.

7. CHAPTER SEVEN- MOBILE SEARCH MARKETING

When we talked about landing pages and Quality Scores in Google Ads, I touched the topic of mobile user experience. The loading speed of a web page on mobile is now officially part of the factors by which Google determines the organic search results ranking.

Mobile Search and its effect on Search campaigns

The keyword quality score is determined by landing page loading time and experience. Once you have some keywords working in your account you can see which they achieve a certain score by simply hovering over their status column. If you see a status alarming of a low Quality Score and hover over you will see the following message:

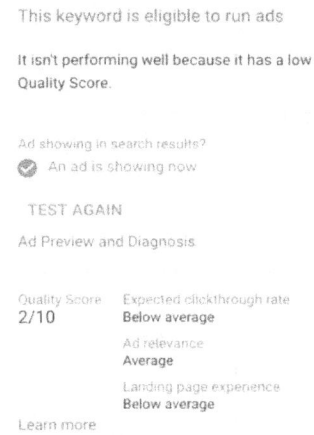

The warning message is activated once your quality score is less than 3 out of 10, which is considered very low.

As you can see the example above, even though this keyword has a decent ad copy attached to it, it has very low expected CTR and Landing page experience. The landing page experience might mean that the page is not related to the search queries, or it loads slowly, or it is not suitable for mobile users.

You can simply check whether the mobile speed of the page is a problem by segmenting the metrics by device:

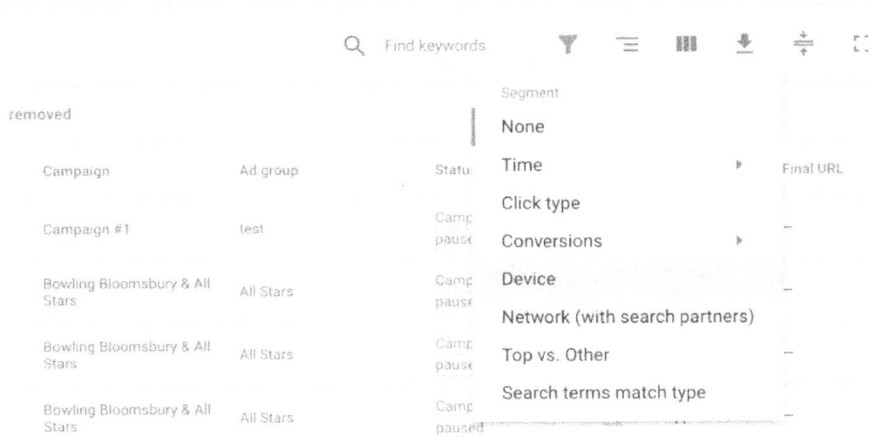

You will then be able to analyse clicks, impressions, conversions on mobile, tablet and desktop devices separately. You can easily see how much a conversion on the mobile device costs you, how is your conversion rate. Significantly more expensive cost per conversion on mobile might indicate problem with the user experience on that type of devices or speed issues.

Google now offers some great columns on how to measure the mobile experience of your landing pages in the new interface. Simply choose Landing Pages from the left-hand side menu.

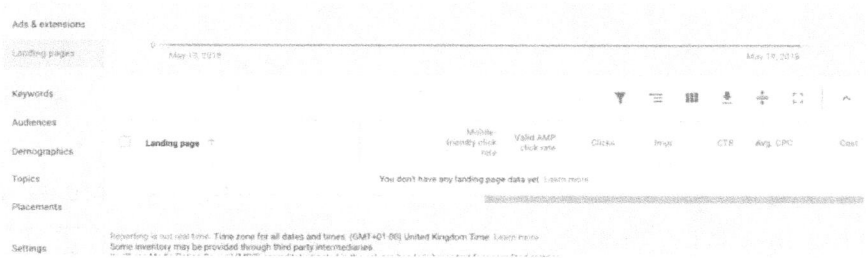

As you can see, the first column is your mobile-friendly click rate. "Mobile-friendly click rate" is the percentage of mobile clicks on the Search Network that go to a mobile-friendly page. If your website is mobile friendly, i.e. it automatically modifies the page to respond to a different screen size, then you will easily be getting 100% here. However this is not solving your problem. You can have a theoretically mobile-friendly website, which is still not very easy to navigate and has a poor user experience.

There are some great ways to check what the actual score of your page on mobile is according to Google. This will help you to determine the problems which you might not know about when reviewing your landing pages.

The first tool you can try is provided by Google and is called Test My Site:

https://testmysite.withgoogle.com/intl/en-gb

You simply enter your landing page URL and you will get a simple report about your speed and experience on mobile.

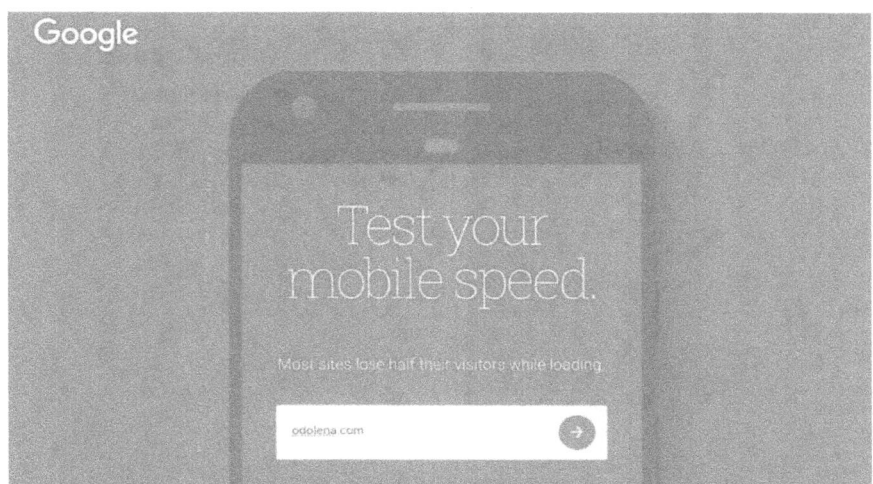

You will then get a score of your page based on the speed of mobile devices. Google takes into consideration the fact that 69% of users connect to the internet via 3G. If your webpage loads slower than 5 seconds, Google considers this borderline performance. According to their studies, you are likely to lose 50% of your visitors if your page loads slower than 5 seconds. Sounds crazy, but think of your own behaviour. How quickly do you exit a website, just because it is not loading? Try counting the seconds of your patience next time.

Another tool which can help you with detecting mobile speed problems and solutions is:

http://www.webpagetest.org/

Test My site is actually powered by this website. What is great about Web Page Test is that you can choose precise geographical location, browser and device. Also, you get much more detailed report.

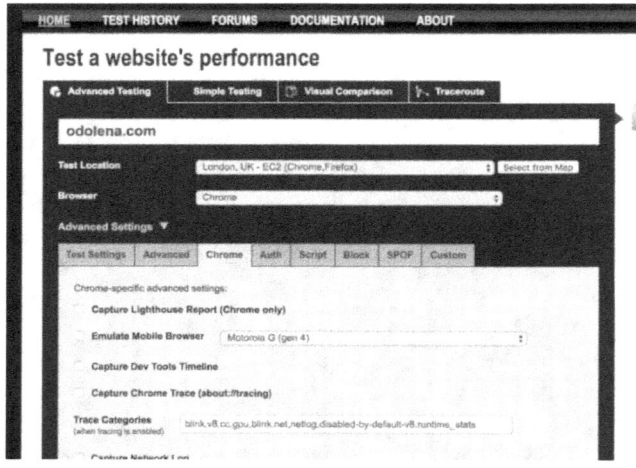

One of the easiest fixes for a slow loading landing page is reducing the image sizes. High-resolution images look good, but do you want to risk your ranking because of a picture nobody saw, because the page was loading too slow?

There are other more technical fixes, which the tools mentioned above will recommend you. This is how a final report looks like:

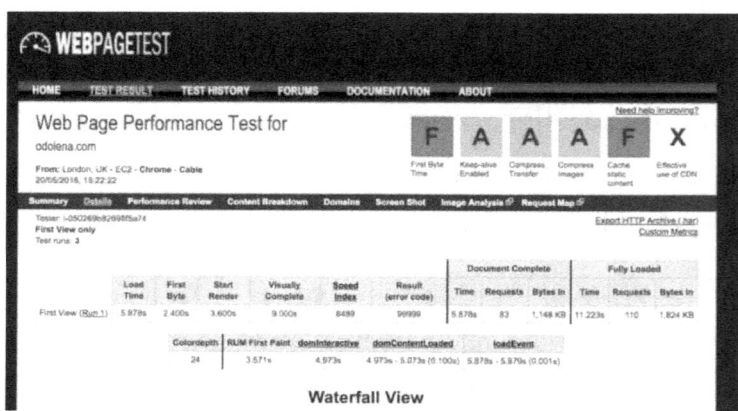

Oh, boy, I scored two F-s for my website Odolena.com. If you click on Image analysis you will be redirected to a more in-detail report which will show you how fine your images are on the A,B,C,D scale and how you can improve them.

Here you can identify images which could be taking way too much space and make the loading process slower. You can simply reduce their resolution and then re-upload them on your page and rerun the test.

AMP (Accelerated Mobile Pages)

AMP is a project started by Google and Twitter aiming to improve the general user experience online. The AMP project launched two years ago and so far has been strongly implemented by the blogging and news industry. As a user you might have spotted the little lightning sign next to a page in a Google search on mobile. If you want your post to appear in the top search results carousel on mobile devices, then the only way is by using Accelerated Mobile Pages.

What are Accelerated Mobile Pages?

AMP is an open-source library that provides a way to create fast-loading mobile-friendly pages. As more and more searches occur on mobile devices the importance of great mobile experience is becoming crucial. Google officially announced that the mobile page loading speed and user experience are taken into consideration for the organic ranking of a website. Many businesses were not ready to invest into turning their websites from mobile responsive to mobile-first. The difference is between a website which is adapting to mobile devices and a website which is designed with the idea to be accessed on mobile most of the time and adapt to desktop when necessary.

To respond to the need for better mobile page experience online, Google collaborated with Twitter to launch the AMP project.

How to implement AMP?

If you are a developer, there are full instructions and documentation on the website of AMP. Google also launched a BETA for some advertisers to get a page they normally drive traffic to with Google AdWords for free. The idea is to prove that an AMP page will outperform any responsive landing page when it comes to conversions and reduce the overall cost/conversion from PPC.

If you are a blogger and are using WordPress, good news for you. You can implement AMP by just activating the official accelerated mobile pages plugin. You can just go to plugins, search for AMP and activate the plugin below:

Once you are done, just test any of your pages by adding /amp/ at the end of the URL and try to open it on a mobile device. The page will open on desktop, too, but to see mobile speed and quality of images, better check on mobile.

AMP and Google Search Console

If you are not using Google Search Console, I would recommend you to connect your website to it. The best about Google Search Console is that it will give you the most popular organic search terms people clicked on and some detailed metrics on organic impressions and clicks.

If you already have connected your website Google Search console, then it will automatically pick up the Accelerated Mobile Pages, once they are created. There is a section called AMP in both the new and the old interface. In both versions, you will see if there are any errors and how many AMPs are already indexed. Google will start indexing the AMP versions of the pages which tend to get most organic traffic first.

You can click on the indexed AMP pages and you will get page details on the side. You will see the code, the canonical URL and if there are any issues. You can also click to test a live version.

The report will give you information about any issues detected and if the page is eligible for the Google Search Results. From here you can submit the page to Google for second indexing. You can view the source code or preview the appearance in search results.

There are three types of search results – Headline, description and image, just headline and image or headline and description. Here are examples of one of my most often displayed articles: The 7 Phases a Successful Online Sales Funnel.

Will AMP improve my SEO?

Mobile speed is officially considered one of the major factors taken into consideration for high organic rankings on Google. Websites which implemented AMP report big increase in organic traffic from mobile devices. Better user experience and high-loading speed are going to influence your website performance positively. Since AMP is a Google's project it is expected to improve the way your website is appearing the organic search results.

Analytics and Tracking AMP results

AMPs found on search are stored and hosted by Google (AMPs on cache), which is on Google.com's domain. When the user clicks a redirecting link on an AMP page they leave the Google domain(Gooogle.com) and come to the domain of the publisher (yourwebsite.com). This person is seen as an external referral, rather than an organic search visitor. This will lead to wrong Google Analytics reports.

You will get to see a lot more sessions because the AMP and the page on which users arrived at will be seen as two separate sessions, instead of one continued. You will see high bounce rate on the AMP pages, as whenever people click a link on them this would be considered an exit. You will therefore see short page duration and low pages per session on AMP pages.

Google was able to implement a fix for this issue in September 2017. If you are using a WordPress extension, you will automatically be connected to the Google Analytics account on your website. You can check this after you have installed the plugin by accessing the Settings and then Analytics. If Google analytics is not enabled, simply tick the box and enter your Google Analytics tracking ID.

What happens then is that data from two different sources are tracked and tied together with a Client ID and you will be able to see what is coming through regular pages vs AMP pages. However, you will not be able to see the difference between Google hosted AMP pages and your own hosted AMP pages. If you are tracking transaction sources you will also see AMP pages as a source with 0 sessions but with transactions.

To solve this problem you can refer to this useful article provided by Stone Temple. What they recommend is first adding ampproject.com to your referrer exclusions. The data from AMP sessions will not be lost, but you will remove the referral (source/medium) over-ride from the user moving from Google.com CDN to your website on the second click. You will be able to see this traffic as google/cpc or google/organic instead as ampproject/referral. This will give you precise information on the improvement of your organic performance after implementing AMP.

8. FACEBOOK ADVERTISING

Facebook is one of the most commonly used social networks in the world with more than 2 billion users. When I talk about Facebook, I don't mean only the Facebook.com website. Similar to Google, Facebook owns many other websites and mobile applications and some of them are also available for advertising.

Very brief history of Facebook

The website was started in 2004 by Marc Zuckerberg and initially was just a platform to connect Harvard students. It was originally called The Facebook and it was one of many other similar networks aiming at university students. Soon it expanded to students from other prestigious universities in the USA and the UK. The platform has now gone far away from its initial audience and is available to everyone.

In 2012 Facebook acquired Instagram, an image sharing service, which allows users to post photos only their smartphone, for 1 billion dollars. In 2014 Facebook acquired WhatsApp, a smartphone instant messaging mobile application, for 19 billion dollars – the highest paid acquisition for a venture-backed startup.

What does that mean for an advertiser?

A lot of people still see Instagram and Facebook as two different platforms. In reality they are very connected. Advertising on Instagram is done through Facebook's Ad Manager. There are many features which are connected in both platforms. You can receive Instagram messages in your Facebook business page inbox. You can see stories(short video posts which disappear after 24 hours) from the people you follow on Instagram. You are notified when your Facebook friends join Instagram. There are much less common features between Facebook and WhatsApp. A lot of people do not even realise that they are the same company now.

Let's go through each of the platforms, owned by Facebook and see what it brings for businesses:

Facebook.com

This is the main platform which you think of when you hear Facebook ads. The Facebook website and mobile application allow connecting people as "Friends" on a personal level and as "Followers" of a company or a brand. All brands must be registered on Facebook as a page, not as a person. Personal accounts which are used as a brand channel are penalised. Also, a personal account has a limit of "Friends" they can have, whereas a company page has an unlimited number of followers and "likes" they can attract.

If you want to advertise on Facebook, Instagram or Messenger, you must have a page. Creating a page is easy and it does not require you to have a registered company. There are a lot of pages which are simply organised by interest.

Facebook also allows creating groups and events which can be great channels for free promotion of your brand. For example, organising an event on Facebook and inviting your customers is a way of engaging and nurturing your community. Sharing your blog articles or company news in relevant groups can help you generate more likes and follows for your page as well as visits to your website.

In this book I will focus solely on the paid advertising on Facebook, as it is one of the easiest and quickest ways of reaching potential customers.

Instagram

Instagram is a mobile application for sharing images with a smartphone device. The website is accessible on a desktop, but the content is created only with a phone.

As Facebook has acquired it, all advertising on Instagram happens through the Facebook for Business publisher's platform. At the moment it is not possible to run ads only on Instagram, you can either run them on both, Facebook and Instagram or only on Facebook.

Comparing Instagram with Facebook, you will realise they are two very different platforms. Where Facebook was designed to be a source of relationship building with your family and friends, Instagram has less privacy. Since recently, you can have a private account, which is not accessible by other users, unless you approve them. Instagram allows users to "like" and comment images and become a follower. As a follower you are notified when users you follow post pictures. Whatever you post on Instagram is available to all your followers and the rest of the world, unless you have a private account. On Facebook, you can limit the number of people you allow to see your posts.

If you want to promote your brand you must use a company Instagram page. If you are already promoting your business from a personal account, you can easily change your personal account to a company page and keep your followers.

People can find your content by using hashtags. These are words and expressions starting with the sign #. This groups the images according to a theme and makes them discoverable. For example, if you write #London with the text accompanying your image on Instagram, this means your image will appear in a group of all the other images which were published with this hashtag. This allows users to discover your profile, like your image or follow you to see more of your future posts.

WhatsApp

WhatsApp is a mobile application for encrypted chat service, image sharing and phone calls. It requires the use of a mobile phone number and a smart mobile device with internet. The fact that it is encrypted means that this information which you shred there is not visible for any of the other websites and mobile applications belonging to Facebook. It is one of the safest ways of sharing private information through the internet.

Advertising on WhatsApp is not possible. There were few occasions when companies were allowed to send a promoted WhatsApp message to people who shared their phone number with them, but generally this is not a very reliable way of marketing.

Messenger

This is the private message service of Facebook, which allows Facebook friends to chat, send images, videos, voice recording or have live video calls. One of the reasons Facebook was in trouble in 2018 was because it became clear that private messages on Messenger were used to collect data about users. For example, Facebook traced what links to websites users share between each other. This information is used to determine interests and behaviour, which can help marketers target people who would be interested in their product.

Messenger is one of the relatively less explored ways of online marketing and Facebook is making some experiments with the platform which will allow brands to engage with users in a very personalised way. To advertise on Messenger, you must have a Facebook page.

Your Facebook company page has the option of automatically welcoming visitors with a personalised private message which is a great way of starting conversations and engaging with customers at their own time. Messenger allows the implementation of simple artificial intelligence-driven chatbot which can provide users with basic information about your service.

Facebook ads is one of the best ways of reaching highly segmented audiences of customers based on their interests. In the spring of 2018 Facebook was investigated because of the data which it collects from its users, which it then "sells" to companies for advertising. I will not go into detail about the moral dispute here; however, the data collected from users is helping us, advertisers, reach the people who are most likely to be interested in our products.

The data which Facebook collects from users' activities online was until recently mapped to other information which they received through partnership with third party data brokers like Epsilon, Acxiom, and Datalogix. This allowed Facebook to create audiences segmented by income. Until recently it was possible to target customers based on their household income in the U.S.A., the U.K. and India. This feature is no longer available after the recent changes in the law for Europe, known as the General Data Protection Regulation (GDPR).

Besides this there are still amazing features of Facebook ads which are much more useful and powerful for advertisers, In the next chapters I will help you create a Facebook ad account and run your first campaign, using some of the most powerful features.

This book is intended for users who have no prior knowledge on Facebook ads, so for those of you who are more advanced, you can skip directly to the chapter after where I explain some more advanced techniques.

Facebook Business Manager

Creating a Facebook campaign is pretty simple and straightforward, but I will lead you through the process as there are some details you should be aware of.

First of all you much have a personal Facebook account as well as a Facebook company page. To create a page, just click on the arrow at the top right corner of your account and choose "Create a Page".

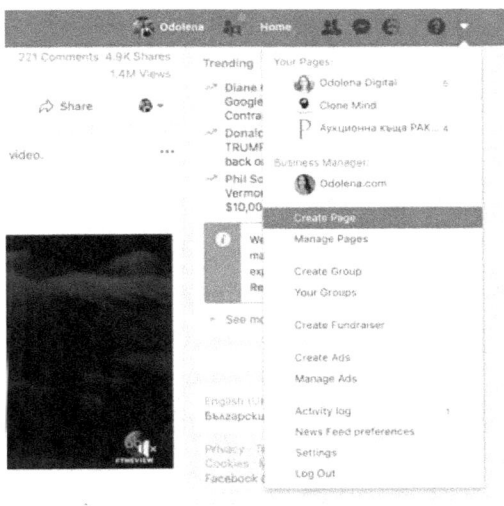

Follow the instructions to create a page for a business, community or a public figure. Then all you need to do is choose profile picture and a background image – same as when you create a personal profile. Now you can start working on your first campaign.

To advertise in Facebook you must create an account with Business Manager. Business Manager is the equivalent of a MCC(My Client Centre) account in Google AdWords. This is a platform which allows you to look after multiple accounts for different clients. In Business Manager, you also have also plenty of settings which allow you to give other people access, control their privileges, assign pages and ad accounts to them. This is also the area where you control your payment methods.

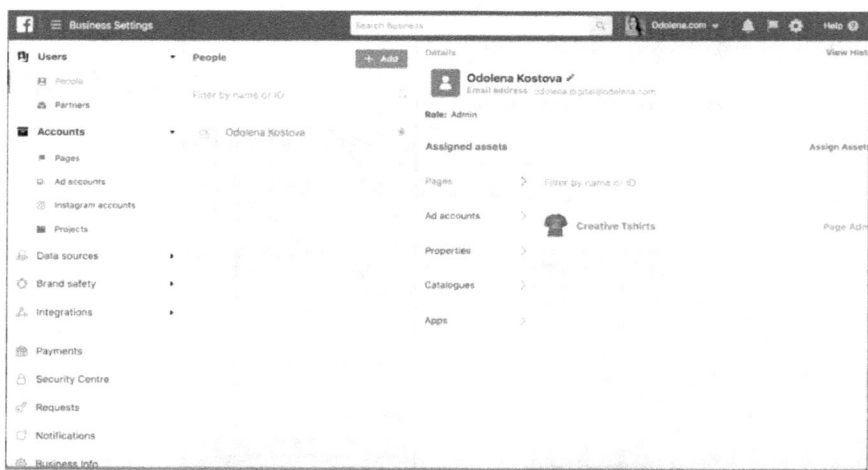

This is the view of your Business Manager home page. The first sections are for adding new users who have access to the account – as people or partners. The first option is more for adding employees or freelancers, where the partner option is for people who have equal contribution rights to yours.

Then in Accounts, you can select pages, Ad accounts, Instagram Accounts or organise projects. If you want to add a new page to My

Business Manager, all you have to do is to click on the blue button "Add". Then you can either take a page you already manage or request access from a client's page. To request access to someone's page, you must already be a manager of at least one business page. This is just the rule – only a page(no personal profile) can request advertising rights from another page. The next step is simply typing in the name or URL of the page you would like to add:

The process is the same for adding other ad accounts and Instagram accounts.

Facebook Pixel

The next section is Data Sources and it is very important. Before digging into it, I have to explain one concept – Facebook Pixel.

This brings us to the next section which is really crucial – Pixels. Facebook Pixel is the equivalent of Google's conversion tracking. If you would like to measure results for your campaigns and optimise them to produce even better results, which you do, you need this. I meet a lot of small businesses which are running paid campaigns without conversion tracking. This makes no sense because you have no idea if your campaigns are working or not. You need to track conversions, no matter what business you have. A conversion can be not only an online sale but a sign-up for a newsletter, opt-in a mailing list, a phone call or an in-store visit.

Setting up a Facebook Pixel is really easy. You can do it yourself or ask for help from the developer who created your website. You only have to name your pixel and choose the option for its installation.

A lot of website platforms like Wix, WordPress, Shopify, Magento, Teespring provide integrations directly with Facebook, which makes the installation very easy.

With WordPress the installation is with a Facebook Pixel Plugin which you have to download from Business Manager(it contains your unique Pixel ID number), upload it in WordPress and activate on your website.

If you would like to install it on a different type of website yourself, you just have to copy the code provided by Facebook and paste it in your header template. In this way the code will be automatically added to all the headers on your website. You can then send test traffic from Facebook to confirm that it works.

If you prefer you can create a custom conversion. This is a very simple and reliable way of tracking results if you redirect customers to a specific Thank You page after a purchase. You can set up different custom conversions at every stage of your funnel, for example, becoming a lead, adding a product to the basket, to a wish list, entered payment information, etc. You can simply enter the URL combination you would associate with this type of action. For example, someone who is a lead, but has not yet added anything to the basket can be a combination of two URLs like the example below:

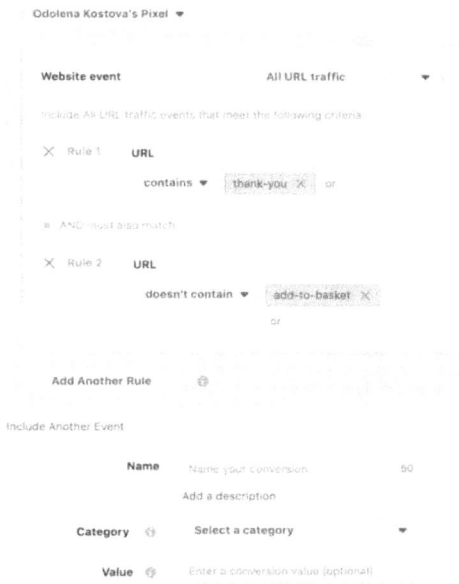

In the Data Sources menu you can also add a mobile application you own. Then you can run an advertising campaign on Facebook, encouraging people to download your application. Users will be directed to the application in App Store or Google Play. There is no need to install Facebook Pixel to track app installs, as the conversions do not happen on your website, but in the App Store or Google Play.

If you want to advertise an e-commerce, you can create a Catalogue of products. This feature will allow your Facebook Pixel to measure online purchases generated by your ads. You can request access to a catalogue which already exists or create a new one. If you decide to create one you can choose between Products, Flights, Hotels,

Destinations, Home Listings and Vehicles. Once you choose a product you have, you must select which pixel you would like to use for the catalogue and you are all set.

Offline events

This is a newer feature of Facebook with the intention to include all possible conversions triggered by an ad. If you are running a campaign which provides users with a code for, let's say, a hotel room discount, you would like to track the people who showed up at the hotel and used their discount code from Facebook. Then you can create an off-line event and simply upload an Excel file with the details of the customers which showed up in person.

If you provide their names, emails, or other information, Facebook will be able to map this to their records. This is useful because then you can choose not to show the ad to them anymore. Even better, you can create a **Lookalike Audience** of Facebook users who have similar interests to the clients who converted already and target them.

Brand Safety

In the Brand Safety you can protect your domain by verifying your ownership to it. This is required in case you suspect someone might be placing ads for your domain.

You can also add Block Lists. A Block List prevents your ads from running on specific websites and apps within the Audience Network, eligible videos of Pages included in the Facebook in-stream placement and specific publishers for the Instant Articles placement.

The next section is Integrations, where you can control who can download the lead collected with Facebook Lead Form ads. I will talk more about Lead Form ads later on, but this is a type of ad which allows users to become your lead by just sharing the email and phone number they used to create their Facebook profile with one click. This tool will allow you to give any person who has a role on the Facebook Page associated with your lead ads, access to download your leads.

In the next section you have to set up your payment method – You can select this also on Ad Account level. You can pay by credit or debit card for your ads and your bill will be a monthly deduction from your account.

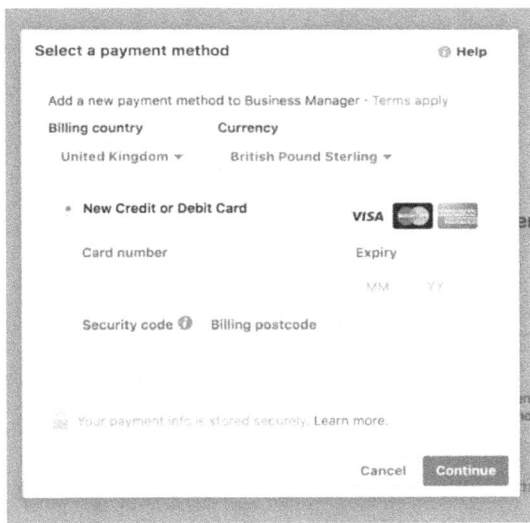

The last sections you will use rarely. The Security Centre will allow you to add another Admin on Business Manager level or increase your security access by asking admins to log in with both email and phone number.

From Requests you can control all the access requests you have received or sent and their approval status. In Notifications, you can select what type of notifications you would like to receive from Business Manager. In Business Info, you can permanently delete your business, change the name, email or Facebook page associated with it. In Set-Up Guide, you have helpful articles about each of the features in the Business Manager account, in case you get stuck.

9. CREATING YOUR FIRST FACEBOOK CAMPAIGN

The next level under Business Manager is the Ad Account, which is usually serving one Facebook page. If you have couple of business lines which have different company pages on Facebook, you must create an Ad Account for each one of them and manger them in Business Manager.

An Ad Account is a container for your campaigns. In Google AdWords you need more levels, because you can only target a certain geography with a single campaign. In Facebook, in each campaign you can have a different Ad Set(the equivalent of an Ad group in Google Ads) which targets a different location with different ads. This allows you to structure the account in a much leaner way. One example:

1. My Business Manager
2. Ad Account for one of my businesses

Campaign 1 for the December Start-Up Business Workshop

Ad set 1 Workshop in London

Ad set 2 Workshop in Leeds

Ad set 3 Workshop in Brighton

Campaign 2 for my upcoming Book

Ad Set 1 Book Premier in London

Ad Set 2 Book Premier in Munich

Ad Set 3 Book Premier in Tokyo

In each Ad set you will have a bunch of ads which call out the exact date and place of the workshop or book premiere event. They show only in the geographic location I have chosen. All of them are scheduled to stop by the date of the event, which is different in each of the cities.

Objectives

This structure allows you to have a lot of flexibility when you are advertising across different geographic locations for different time periods, but have one objective. Objectives can be selected only on the Campaign level. There are three groups of Objectives:

1. **Awareness**

In the Awareness type of campaign you can choose between **Reach** and **Brand Awareness**. There is a slight, but very important difference. Brand Awareness will optimise your campaign to show to people who are likely to recall your product from a Facebook ad they have seen. This is called the "ad recall lift" delivery optimisation.

If you go for Reach, Facebook will try to show your ad to as many people as possible within your chosen audience and show it very frequently. You can set up caps on how many impressions and restrict the audience by geography, demographics, interests and other factors on Ad Set level.

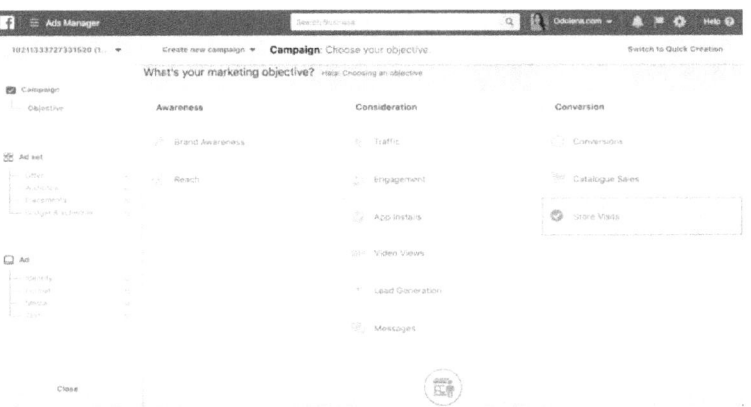

2. Consideration

In the Consideration section you have campaign objectives focused more on specific actions you would like your prospects to take. The first option is **Traffic**, which is purely getting people to go to your website, application or Messenger. In Google there is the same type of campaign – optimising for Web Traffic. **Engagement** is a campaign type which will try to show your ad to people who are likely to interact with the ad itself, rather than click on it. These are audiences which are proven to comment, share, like, react to posts more often. Engagement on your ad can increase your visibility – the more social actions on an ad, the more people are likely to see it. You have probably seen some ads with a small text from Facebook on top: Your friend XYZ likes this. This is the effect of high engagement.

App Installs as you can imagine will allow you to direct people to your mobile application in Apple App Store or Google Play.

Video Views will show your ads to people who are keen video watchers. Obviously, your ad type must be a video to use this function.

Lead Generation is one of the most commonly used objectives. It corresponds to the Leads type of campaign in Google. There is one major difference; the **Lead Ad** will pre-populate the sign-up form with the users' Facebook account name and email. All they have to do then is agree and they get in your lead list in Facebook automatically. This is a great strategy if you don't have a landing page to collect leads. You can then download the details of the people who signed up and import them in your CRM.

Messages is a unique type of campaign which is something I have seen a few people experimenting with yet. It encourages people to send private messaged to your campaign. This could be a great option if you are using a chatbot for Facebook. Such a campaign with an automated conversation can easily be used to collect leads, too. For example, it can first introduce a product and then ask for the user's email to send them more information. This is all possible with automated chat bot systems.

3. **Conversions**

The first option is called **Conversion** and it is very similar to the Lead Generation type, but in this case you will direct people to a landing page. The Pixel you have installed in Business Manager will record a conversion whenever someone reaches the URL you have selected(for example, Thank You page after a sign up).

Catalogue Sales is the type of campaign for e-commences. In Business Manager, you can create a catalogue for your products and set up a purchase pixel to fire whenever a sale is executed.

Offline Sales is where the data you upload from people who did an offline transaction or valuable action will come in handy. Facebook will optimise to show to people who are near the brick-and-mortar locations of your business. Also you can create a similar audience to the offline customers you have uploaded and optimise the campaign even further

Ad sets in Facebook

The Ad Set is the place where you will make the most significant settings and changes. In Facebook Ad Sets have the sophistication of a campaign in Google AdWords. This is the place where you determine your geographic targeting, audiences, budget and schedule.

The first section will be different depending on the type of campaign you have chosen. If it is a Video Views, Engagement or Awareness type of campaign you will be directed to choose your audience settings. The other types require some more specifications:

If your objective is Traffic, you must specify where you want the traffic to come to – your website, an app or your company page's Messenger.

If you have selected App Installs as an objective, you must specify which App, which store, in which countries it is available and add a URL linking to it. If you have many apps, you can select to show a catalogue. This will allow Facebook to show the best product for each particular user, based on their interests and online behaviour.

If your objective is Lead Generation, you just have to specify your landing page as a next step. If you like you can also add a catalogue, you can do this too.

Messenger Ad Sets

For the Messages objective you can choose whether you would like to initiate conversations by encouraging people to click on the ad in the news feed(Click to Messenger), or you would rather directly message your target audience with an ad (Sponsored messages).

The Sponsored Messages type is one of the most innovative ad types Facebook offers. On the 2018 annual conference Facebook introduced some really interactive message ads they launched with brands like Sephora and Nike. Features like phone camera and filters can turn such an ad into a really immersive experience. For example, Sephora designed a filter which allows users who get the message to try different makeups on their face by using their Messenger video camera:

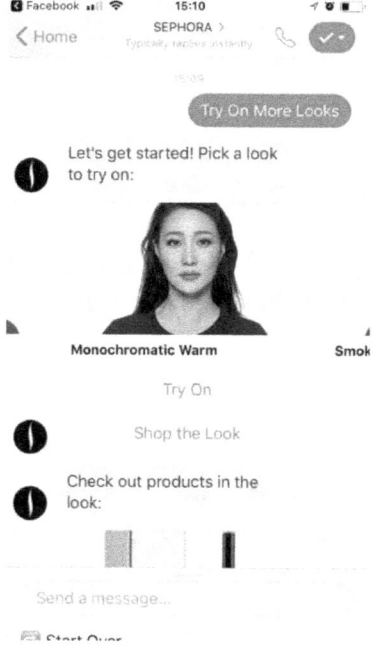

If the user selects "Try on" Messenger will activate the mobile camera and apply the makeup to a face it detects. Then users are offered to order the makeup used for this look.

This is a super exciting feature, even though not available yet for all businesses. There are a lot of creative ways to use messages for advertising without getting intrusive.

Conversion Ad Sets

If you have chosen the Conversion objective, you must specify what type of conversion pixel you need. Pixels for a filling out a form, adding a product to a basket or a conversion in Messenger are different. If your conversion is an App install, you must add an App in Business Manager and select it here(See previous chapter).

You can run a Catalogue Sale ad set to sell products directly online. You can choose all products or create a product set for your campaign. A product set is a group of products you can organise by factors like category, brand, price, etc.

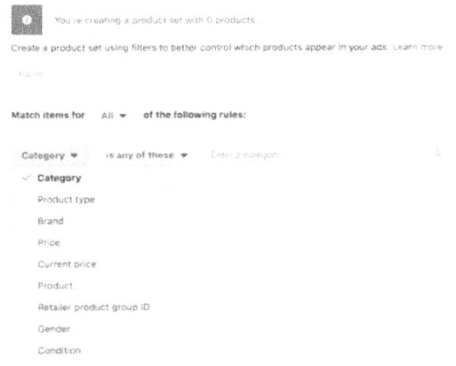

Facebook also allows you to optimise for a Store Visit. To use this conversion, you must set up a Business Location in Business Manager. This is the equivalent of setting up a location on Google Maps. In this way Facebook can optimise and show your ad to people who are physically near your store's location.

Offer Ad Sets

If you are building a conversion type of campaign (Conversion, Catalogue Sales, Store Visit), you can optionally create an offer. This can be online only or also in-store offer. You can schedule the time when users will see the offer. Also, you can create promotional coupon codes, or upload your own unique ones. Offer ads will appear as newsfeed promoted content, notifications or an email reminder if a user chooses to save the ad.

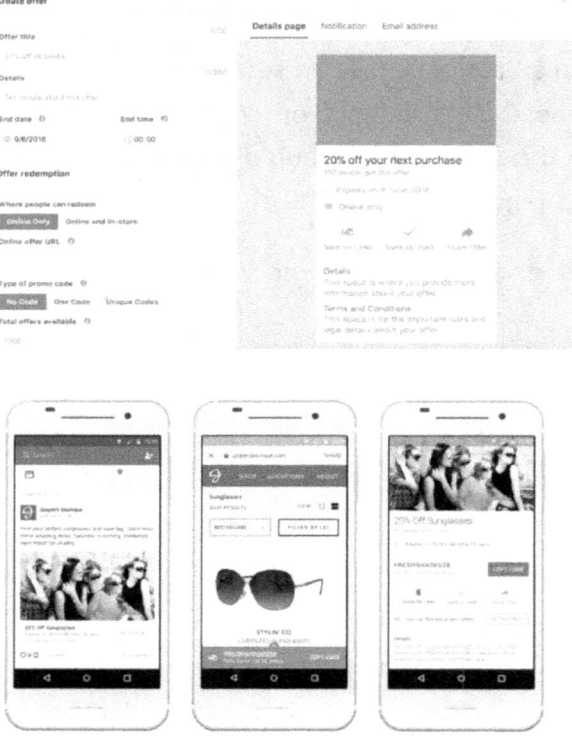

Here are examples of the different formats of offer ads:

Audiences

This is one of the most important parts of an Ad Set creation. The audience definition is the main targeting of your ad. This together with your ad creative will be the main factors for the success of your campaigns.

Custom Audiences

Custom audiences are the most powerful tool Facebook has right now for advertisers. There are two types of custom audiences – Remarketing and Lookalike. Here is how to create them.

A Custom audience can be based on website page users have visited on your website, customer file, app installation, in-store visit or engagement with your content. All these can be tracked to a unique Facebook user who will be shown your ad! To start building an audience, click on "Create an Audience" in the Ad Set builder. You will get this menu:

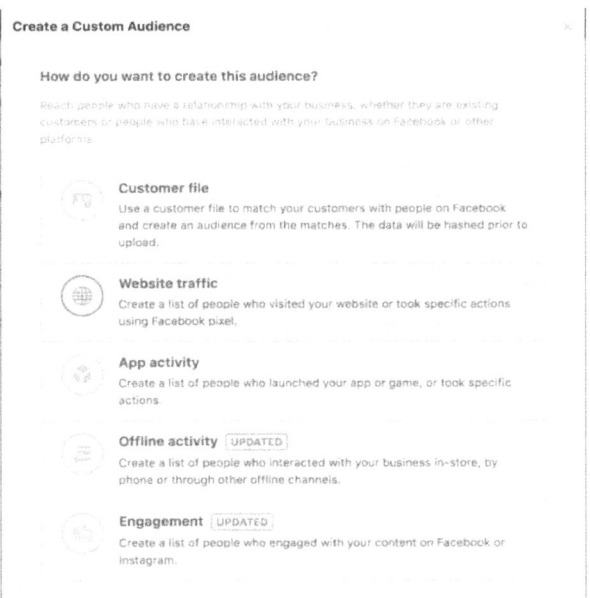

As you can see, there are different types of Audiences you can build here – website visitors, email list uploads, app activity, offline activity(also a customer list) and engagement.

To create a Custom Audience, choose Customer File and upload an Excel spreadsheet with the names, emails, phones, countries or Zip codes of your customers. This information will be mapped against the user database of Facebook. In this way you can target very precisely only people who have bought a certain product from you, or attended an event, signed up for more information, etc.

The minimum list size is 30 names. Of course, the more you provide, the higher chance for Facebook to make a match. Once you have uploaded the file it will take a few hours to populate the list and then you can get an estimation of how many matches were found.

Lookalike Audiences

Once you have uploaded a customer list of emails, you either target these people or ask Facebook to create a list of unknown to your users, who are similar to the ones you have just uploaded. This type of audience is called a Lookalike.

How does Facebook define which users to include in a Lookalike audience? There are many signals users leave while using Facebook – pages and posts they have liked, companies they follow, even other ads they have previously engaged with. One of the biggest arguments against Facebook Lookalike audiences and generally any audience segments they have built is that they use declared interests, rather than the real ones. Someone who likes a page about sports cars, might not be in the position to buy one.

With this thought in mind, you must know although Lookalike audiences can expand your reach to a whole pool of new prospects, it can also easily bring you a lot of vaguely interested people.

Have in mind that behaviour varies across countries. If you have uploaded a customer list of UK users and what to create a lookalike audience to target Russia, you might not reach the right people.

Also, when uploading the list, you can choose whether you would like to have the top 1% of lookalike matches – the ones that are closest to your original list or to go broader. The broader you go the larger and less lookalike your audience becomes. When I run campaigns, I rarely expand over 1%. It is OK, to go over 1%, if your audience is small and you want to increase your reach. However bear in mind that the users you will reach might be quite different from your ideal customer.

Other Audiences

The other audiences you can build are very similar to what you can have in Google AdWords, which I already explained in the previous chapter. The **Website Traffic** audience is a remarketing list generated with a tag on your website. You can create an audience of users who have been on a certain page of your website and have not been on another, for example. The **App Activity** can remarket people who have:

Installed your app

Recently opened your app

Recently completed a purchase

Completed large purchases

Achieved a certain level in your game

The Engagement audience is an interesting type of audience, which is based on activities the users have taken on your Facebook page.

When you select this type of audience, you have a list of actions you could build your audience on – time spent watching your video, filled out a Lead form, used canvas experience(full screen type of ads, which we will cover in the next chapter), interaction with your Facebook or Instagram page or an event you have created.

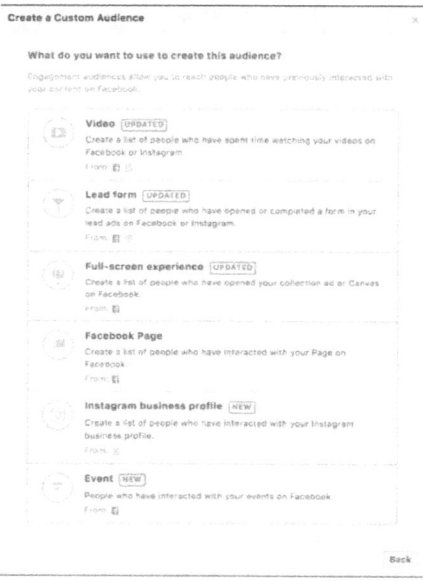

Facebook ads

When creating a Facebook, you have mainly two choices – to boost an existing post from your page, or to create an ad from scratch. What is the difference? Creating a new ad gives you access to all the ad types available. If you are boosting a current post, you only expand the reach of your post to more users, outside of your followers.

Let's dive into the different ad types:

Single Image and Single Video ad

The Single Image ad is very straightforward. You select an image and add text above it, a Headline and a small text under the image. It typically looks like a sponsored post on your page. The difference between boosting a post you have shared and creating single image ad is that the ad you created will not show on your Facebook page. It will look like a post you shared, but it will only exist as an ad. A boosted post will stay on your page, as well as show as an ad.

For example this post from Google cannot be found on their Facebook page. It is an ad promoting an event in, which is shown to a selected audience.

Full-Screen Experience

This is also known as a Canvas ad. It looks like a standard image ad, but when a user interacts it expands to a full-screen animation or video. This type of ad is available only for mobile devices. There are some existing templates you can use, or you can create your own HTML ad and upload it.

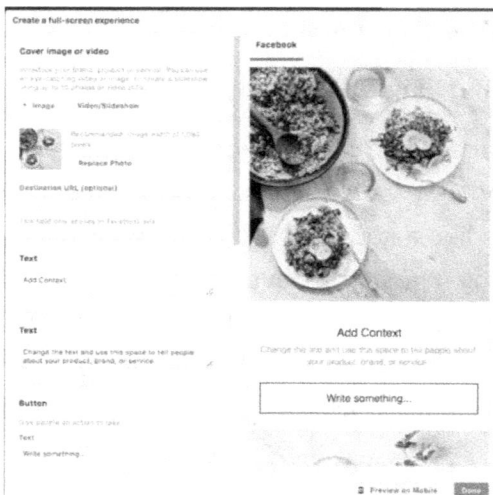

Here is an example of a "Get New Customers" template. You can replace the images with videos and provide a whole experience by scrolling.

Canvas can be a great way to attract customers with an inspiring creative. The ad is quite easy to make with a template and a few good images.

Slideshow ad

This type of ad includes several images, with a call to action. It is great if you would like to show several products. Users get to engage with the carousel, by clicking on the arrows to see the next image. On each of the slides users can click on a button to take them to a landing page.

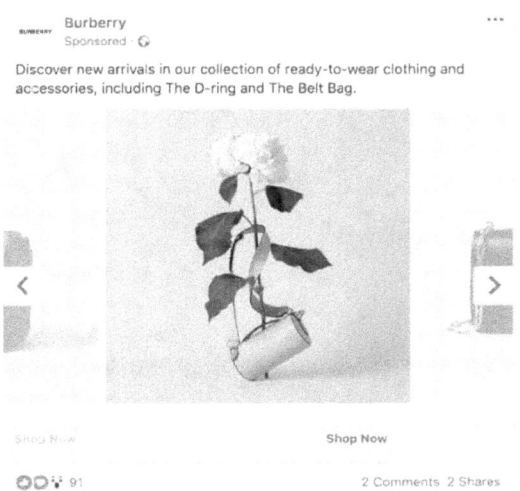

Here is an example of a Slideshow ad, which is widely used by fashion brands on Facebook.

Lead Ads

When talking about campaign objectives, I mentioned about the lead ad form, it is an ad type which does not redirect to a landing page. It allows the user to subscribe or fill out a form in Facebook, with the email other information, they have already provided. To set up lead ads, you must first do this in the Business Manager. You must use some kind of a CRM(Customer Relationship Management). This is a place where you collect all the customer data like emails, phone numbers and notes. There are many on the market depending on how sophisticated you need it to be. If you are just collecting emails, you can use something as simple as Mailchimp. It allows you to send automated emails and collect data in different lists.

Most CRMs have an integration with Facebook through an API. This way the people who fill out the form, go directly in your database. Connecting a CRM with Facebook works through a solution called Zapier. To make the connection, must go to your Facebook Business page, choose Publishing tools and the Lead set up.

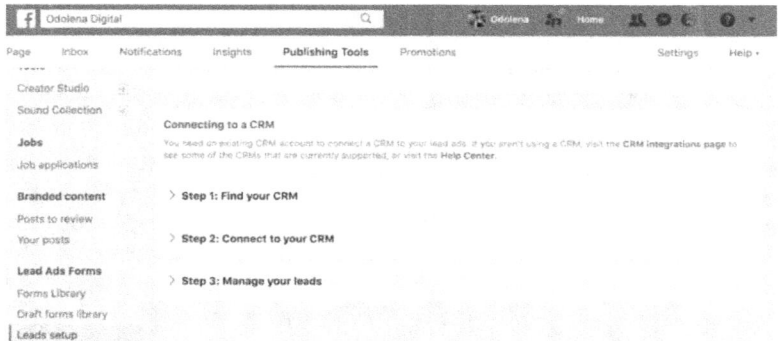

Find your CRM, follow the instructions to connect and then finish.

Once you have done this, create a Campaign with Lead objective. When you are at the ad creating stage, you will see a section to add a lead form. Create a new one. You can choose whether you would like to make it very easy to fill out or indicate a stronger buyer intent. The second option includes an extra step where the user has to review their information before they submit the form.

Lead ads can easily generate a huge amount of leads, which have a vague interest or buying intention. This is why you must decide what is more important for you – quality or quantity. Even with the review step, you will generate a lot of leads, so be careful with your audience.

Here is how a lead form set up looks like:

You can customise the form according to the needs of your business. A nice image on top, combined with a strong headline can increase your chance of success.

10. THE GOOGLE DISPLAY NETWORK

The Google Display Network is a network of websites which partner up with Google to show ads of third-party advertisers. The tool they use is called Google AdSense. In the ecosystem of online advertising such websites are called publishers. Where Facebook can act as its own publisher as it owns the platform, Google has to partner up with websites which generate traffic by themselves and would like to make money from it. Whenever an advertiser on the GDN is charged (either per click or per thousand impressions), part of the cost is paid to the website and another part to Google.

What is the Google Display Network?

Every time a user clicks on a display ad published in the Google Display Network (GDN), the advertisers are charged per click, similar to the way search ads work. However, with Google Display a portion of this click is received by the website where the ad was displayed.

The ads are shown in spaces between the content of the websites called placements. Each website decides how many placements they would like to have per page. The total amount of placements is called inventory. Websites can sell their inventory by number of impressions(or times the ad has been displayed) where the cost is usually per 1000 impressions. They can also sell by cost per click. Many big websites sell their best inventory by signing a deal with the advertiser directly without a middleman like Google.

In fact, in the past all online advertising was sold by cold calling and making individual contracts with every advertiser. However this brought a lot of hassle for both, advertisers and publishers and a lot of inventory left unsold. This is when Google saw the opportunity to act as a mediator helping websites to make the most of the available inventory and advertisers to have immediate access to thousands of websites on various topics all over the world.

Now only the top inventory of very popular websites is sold individually to the advertiser. However even websites like Forbes and CNN end up with a lot of unsold inventory which they distribute through display networks like Google. This means that any advertiser out there can secure their ad to be displayed on some of the biggest publishers' websites. This doesn't involve cold calling, travelling to meet editors, negotiating – it is just on your fingertips.

Creating a GDN Campaign

It has never been easier to create ads for the Google Display network. To start, just get to Campaigns and click the Plus button. Choose Display, then you can choose what the goal of your campaign. Then you can choose between Gmail and Standard display. I will show Gmail campaign in the next chapter, so for now choose Standard display and enter your website URL.

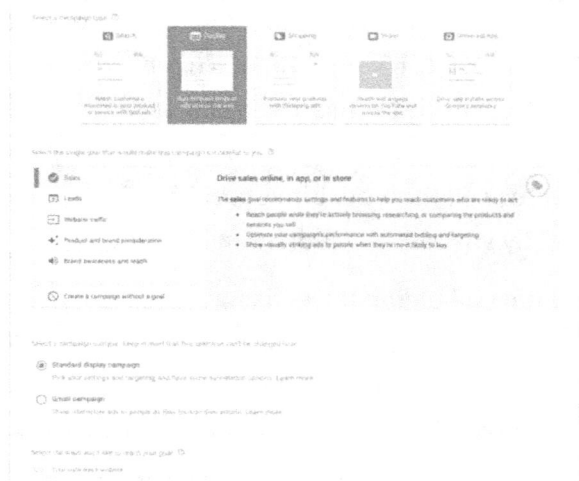

Then you go through pretty much the same Settings process like you did when creating a search ad - naming your campaign, selecting a location, language and a daily budget.

When it comes to selecting a bidding strategy one of the unique ones is Viewable CPM. If with display you want to optimise for viewable impressions, i.e. times when your ad appeared in the viewable fold of the page – so the user actually was exposed to the ad. On the side you can see how the audience size potential changes depending on the bidding strategy I choose.

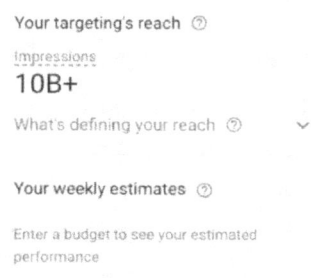

One great benefit of advertising with the GDN is that you do not need a long history with AdWords to optimise for conversions. This is very important for search campaigns. For display, all the history is on domain level, so if your website's domain has a good history of a lot of conversions, you can try an automated strategy. Google will easily optimise on the past performance of the website.

In this case, I choose Select a bid strategy directly. Then the least automated strategy is manual CPC and I am going to tick the box for enhanced CPC. ECPC looks for ad auctions that are more likely to lead to conversions and then raises your max CPC bid (after applying any bid adjustments you've set) to compete harder for those clicks. If a click seems less likely to convert, AdWords will lower your bid. ECPC will try to keep your average CPC below the max CPC you set (including bid adjustments) but may exceed your max CPC for short periods of time.

Ad Rotation

I would suggest choosing "Optimise – Choose Best Performing Ads". Powered by Google's machine learning technology, the "Optimize" setting prioritises ads that are expected to perform better than other ads within an ad group.

Then you can add some schedule such as when you want your ad to appear, when you want to finish the campaign if it has an end date. What devices you would like to appear on, operating systems, device models, networks.

Frequency

This is an essential feature for display advertising. You can have a cap on how many times people see the ad per day. I would recommend you always put some kind of an appearance cap. You can set this up per day, per week and then per ad group or campaign.

You would like to appear in front of a large audience, not only in front of the same people over and over again. This can not only get people annoyed for seeing the same ad over and over again, but it can make them "immune" to your message. Also you are risking to pay a lot more for reaching the same people multiple times.

Nowadays, there are ad-blocking extensions which people install on their browser. Also Google extended the websites and apps covered by its network on which users can choose to block an advertiser. This happens with a small close sign in the top right corner of the ad. When pressed you get the following message:

Users can choose to report you if they see the ad inappropriate in any way. Also they can complain they have seen it too often, it is not relevant to them, etc.

Google collects these complaints and if you get too many your ad performance might be severely affected. This is why it is crucial to put good quality ads, show them to a relevant audience and put cap on your views.

Content exclusions

You can exclude certain website categories of web content so your ad does not appear there. You can choose on the way the content is labelled – similar to the movie labelling websites are also labelled depending on what audience the content is for.

Content exclusions can protect your ads of showing on inappropriate pages, but also increase your bid when overdone.

Then you can exclude all kind of sensitive content. I will do this if I do not want my brand associated with such content. If you want to be cautious, you can exclude this type of content.

In the content type, you might want to take out "Games". The problem with these impressions is that it is very likely that you get clicks by mistake while people are navigating through an app and you will have to pay for them. Games and mobile application impressions can be very valuable if your landing page is well optimized for mobile devices.

You can also exclude "below the fold" impressions. This is when your ad appears on a location, where users have to scroll down to see it. If they don't scroll down you will have an impression counted on this website, but it will not be viewable. So if you don't opt out of this you must make sure you always check your viewable CTR in the reports (i.e. viewable impressions/clicks), as you might be misguided by having a very low CTR otherwise.

There are few options only valid for YouTube – in live streaming, in video(i.e. in the middle of a video), embedded video – when YouTube video is on someone else's website. These are quite intrusive times to show an ad, so you can opt-out if you are doing a video campaign.

11. AUDIENCES ON GOOGLE DISPLAY

Once you are on ad group level, you can start building your audiences. Audiences are on ad group level for display so that you can run several different ad groups targeting different groups of users with a different creative.

After you name your first ad group you will see this Audience section:

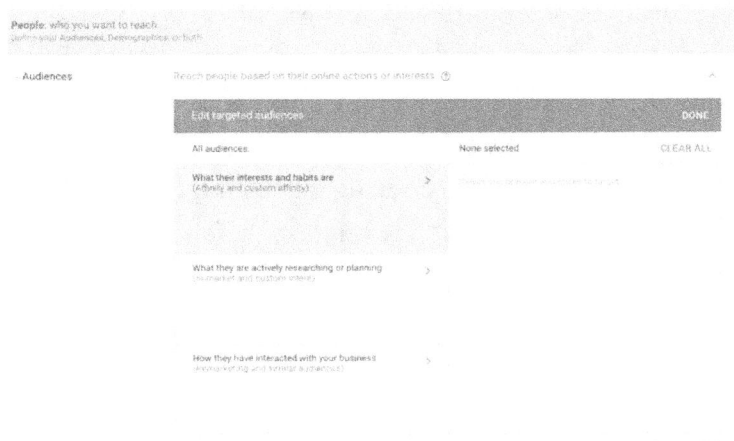

The Audience builder in Google AdWords

In the section you have six different types of audiences you can create, summed into easy to understand buckets. The first one is based on interests – Affinity and Custom Affinity. There are ready segments built by Google based on the activity of people online and also the opportunity to build your own segments by the criteria which define your own users.

The second group is summed under what users are actively researching and planning and the audiences available are In-market segments and Custom Intent. These are similar to Affinity and Custom Affinity, but instead of general interest, the users in these groups have shown buying intent in their behaviour.

The last option is summed under how users interacted with your business. In this bucket, you have remarketing lists and similar audiences. These are either people who have been on your website or people who have very similar online activity. We will go through each type of audience and explain their pros and cons.

Affinity audiences and Custom Affinity

The first option from the list is affinity audiences or custom affinity. These are broader segments and you will often discover they seem to be more related to online content consumer, rather than online purchasing activity. You can see that they group users according to hobbies, entertainment preferences, interest. The problem is that, for example, people who like cooking videos might be in the healthy food in-market segment, but they might be a falling into many other different categories.

In most cases, I would not recommend you to target only Affinity Audiences. To make sure you have a relevant audience, I would always combine affinity with something else which I know about my customers. Try a combination of visitors of certain URL on your website who are also fans of luxury travelling, for example.

You can also analyse other audiences you have created in the Audience Insights report in AdWords and see, for example how many of your website visitors are Keen Cooks or Sports Junkies. This information can help you create a customer persona. I will go into more detail about the Audience Insights Report in the next chapters.

You can also see the option to create your own Custom Affinity Audience which is a combination of affinity category – URL, places, apps. For example, rather than reaching the Sports Fans affinity audience, a running shoe company may want to reach Avid Marathon Runners instead. With custom affinity audiences, the shoe company can further define this audience by:

- Entering interests like 5K in San Francisco, triathlon athlete, or long-distance runner

- using URLs of websites with content about running, training schedules, marathon nutrition, and other marathon themes

- entering places that an Avid Marathon Runner might be interested in like gyms, sporting goods stores, and natural supermarkets, or

- entering apps in the Health & Fitness category that an Avid Marathon Runner may likely be interested in like Google Fit.

In-Market Segments and Custom Intent

The second category is In-Market Segments. Like Affinity Categories In-Market Segments are predefined by Google based on the behaviour of users online. However, the focus here is on people who are ready to make a purchase. Users typically stay in an In-Market Segment no more than 24 hours. In this period, they either make a purchase of the product they were defined in a segment for, or they are removed from the In-Market Segment. The reason is that Google wants to have an audience of people who are presumably searching to make a purchase.

When you browse through the In-Market segments you will see a variety of very niche products. It gets as granular as the product categories on Amazon if you take a look. Just if you take the jewellery section, you will see this is divided into three smaller segments – Fine Jewellery, Watches, Wedding and Engagement Rings.

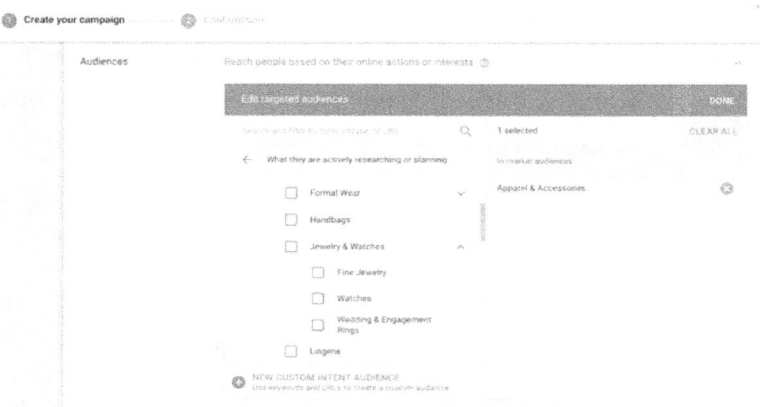

In-Market Segments help advertisers find active buyers for a product type

You would wonder where Google gets all the information from. It is generated from millions of micro-interactions which are detected as signals for someone's interest in a product. Because Google has such a wide variety of online products, it can gather the exact amount of signals. These are some of the products which could have been used to create In-Market segments. I do not claim that all of them are used to give away our precious personal data; however, Google does collect signals from many of its products.

Here is a list of the products owned by Google, just to give you an idea of how large this company is and how many opportunities these products deliver to learn about people's behaviour online. I do not claim Google uses information from all of them; however, I was not able to find a clear statement that it doesn't either.

- A **Google search**, containing "buy", "near me", "cost" etc. Every salesman will tell you these are buying questions.

- A visit of a shop or exposition detected on **Google Maps**. You know when you leave a hotel, you get a message from Google Maps: "How was the Crown Plaza?" Combined knowledge about when, where and how long people spend time physically and online can pretty much tell you everything about them. Depending on your settings you can exclude Google from seeing your physical location, but most people are unaware.

- **Google Flights** provide priceless information on peoples travel plans and locations of interest. This is great for any businesses trying to attract incoming tourists before they have even left their home country.

- Watching a **YouTube** product review or unboxing. This is a clear signal that this person is very likely to buy such type of product soon.

- Installing an app in **Google Play**. A lot of apps give valuable information about what is important for you right now. A woman getting an app about fertility prediction is very likely trying to get pregnant.

- If you are using an **Android** device your device periodically contacts Google servers to provide information about your device and connection to their services. This information includes things such as your device type, operator name, crash reports and which apps you've installed.[4]

- Spending time on certain websites, using **Google Ad Sense**. Someone frantically checking laptop prices on technology stores' websites is very likely to be a buyer.

- Blogs. Don't forget the **Blogger** platform is also owned by Google – all comments, engagements and follows you have there are signals, too.

- **Gmail.** This is a bit of grey territory, as Google has one privacy policy for all its products and it does not really mention whether data from personal emails in its mail product is used. All I saw in the privacy policy is that *activity information that Google collects may include people with whom you communicate or share content*.[5]

- **Google +** which is not as popular as other social media, but it still provides some signals about online behaviour like shares, Google + button clicks and comments.

- **Google Hangouts** – this video conference call system for texting and making phone calls. **Google Voice** app gives you a free phone number for calling, text messaging, and voicemail. Google may collect telephony log information such as your phone number, calling-party number, receiving-party number, forwarding numbers, time and date of calls and messages, duration of calls, routing information and types of calls.[6]

---

[4] https://policies.google.com/privacy?hl=en-GB&gl=uk#infocollect
[5] https://policies.google.com/privacy?hl=en-GB&gl=uk#infocollect
[6] same as 5

- **Google Translator** – something simple as a translation of words can also provide valuable information about someone's online activity.

- Of course, the often use of marketing tools like **Google AdWords, Google Trends, Google Search Console** gives a clue about the professional interest of a user.

- The **Google Pixel** phone the Chromebook laptops which store all files on **Google Drive**

- Shopping behaviour on **Google Shopping** as well as on new smart gadgets like **Google Home**, **Chromecast** and **Nest**.

If you are already blown away, don't worry – being aware of all this can help you be smarter about your activity online. It can also give you an idea about the huge opportunities the access to this network gives you as a marketer.

Besides the pre-built In-market Segments, Google has auto created a Custom Intent audience for you based on your URL. This is basically an In-Market segment built precisely for your business. It will automatically generate lists of display keywords based on the content on your website.

For example, I entered the website of a well-known U.K. car comparison platform called www.carwow.co.uk, which allows people to browse deals from dealerships all over the country. Below you can see the list of display keywords which Google generated for me based on the content of the website.

Custom Intent audience building based on a website URL – an array of suggested keywords appears as ideas based on the content of the site.

This is very similar to the Keyword Planner which we used to generate keywords for our search campaigns. Display keywords work differently compared to search keywords. Here are the main differences:

- Display keywords target your ads to appear on websites which have content related to the keywords, or target users who have previously shown interest in the context of this keyword via some the Google-owned platforms I mentioned above.

- Display keyword has no matches – they only provide a context of the type of user you want to target or the type of website you would like your ad to show on.

- They can be long and specific, which will not affect the number of impressions your ad receives. Whereas for Search, it is a matter of sticking balance of a good search volume, relevancy and low completion, on Display, you can go as niche as you like – it gets only better.

In any case you can easily evaluate the size of your audience in the same tool. Remember that these are just estimations and can vary a lot, depending on how precise your targeting requirement is.

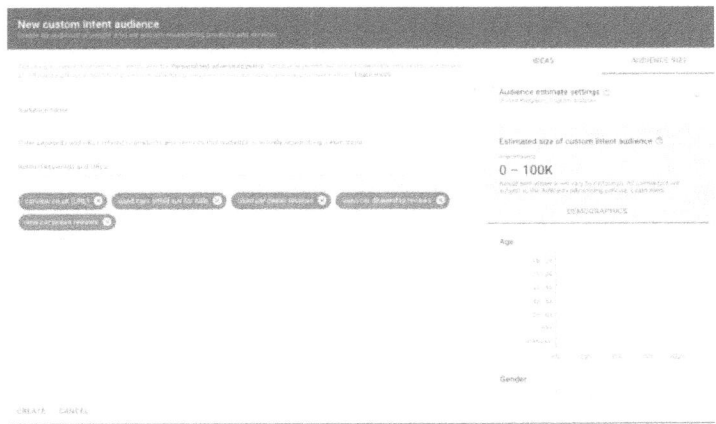

Filling in your settings with keywords and URLs until you start getting large enough estimated audience.

In the example of carwow.co.uk, I was not able to generate anything concrete – just an estimation anywhere between 0-100 k. When you see this kind of estimation, it might be worth adding more keywords and also other websites. The more context you give to Google, the better-defined audience definition you are going to get.

How to check what Google thinks you are interested in?

There is a way to see how Google has classified you according to your web activity and why. To see this go to your personal account. If you are using Google Chrome, you can click on your picture in the top right corner of the screen and select My Account.

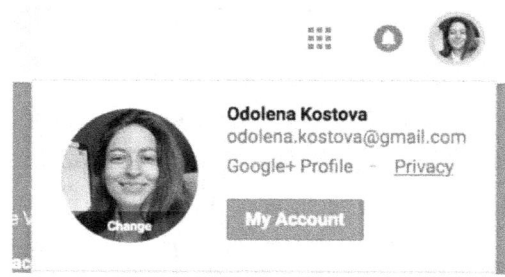

If you are on another browser like Mozilla, Safari, Internet Explorer, just go to https://myaccount.google.com/

Then, once you have signed in, you will see a lot of options which give you control on how Google can use your data and the level of privacy you want to have. Choose Ad Settings in the Personal Info & Privacy.

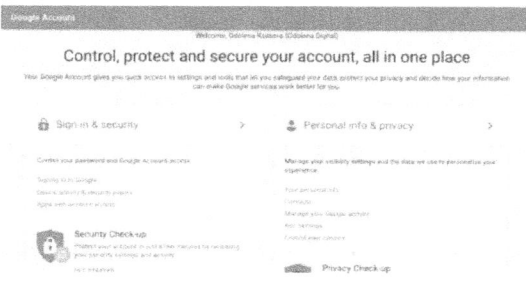

Then select Manage Ad Activity.

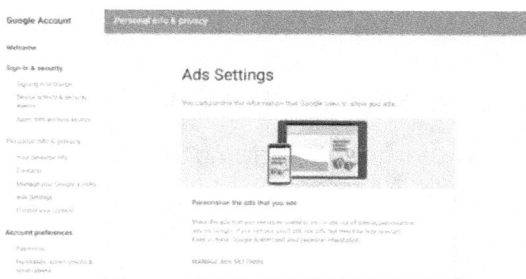

Here you can see if your Ad Personalization is on or off. If it is on, this means that you have allowed Google to collect information from your online behaviour on Google's owned platforms to help advertisers show you relevant to your interest's ads. If you click on more options you will see a tick box which allows Google to collect such data about you also on their Partner's Network which we mentioned in the beginning of this chapter. These are all the websites which use Google Ad Sense to allow Google Display ads to show n their inventory and earn money form this activity.

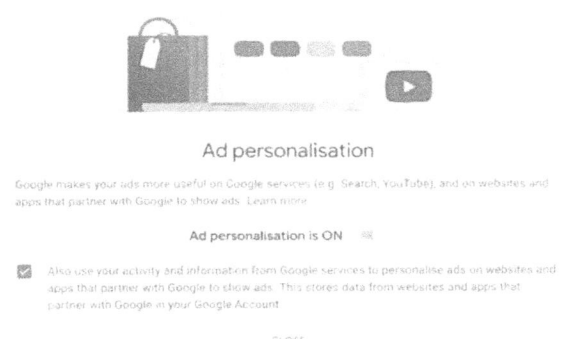

You can switch ad personalisation off if you do not want Google to show ads based on your online history.

You can see a section called *How Your Ads Are Personalised?* This will allow you to learn about what Google thinks you are interested in and why.

This is different from cookies. Cookies are collected by websites to understand their customers' behaviour by attaching a unique string of numbers to their browser. I will explain exactly how this works when we talk about Remarketing. Some of the companies Google thinks you are interested in might have also dropped a cookie in your browser if you visited their website. However, these are just companies Google has identified you are interested in from your online behaviour on Google's platforms and Google Partners' websites.

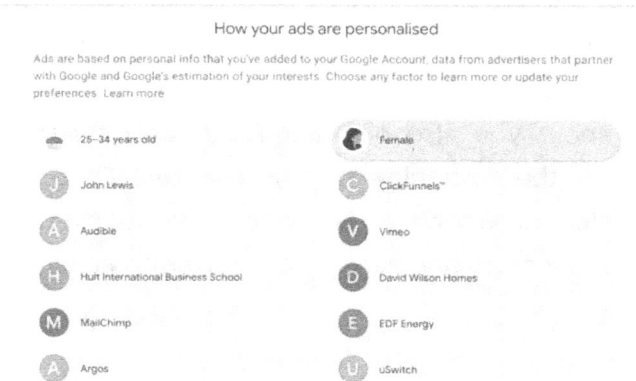

Here is a snapshot of what Google thinks about me:

This is quite accurate as I indeed fall into the right Age and Gender group and have engaged with all the websites mentioned recently. If I click on any of the icons, I see from where Google has received this data. For example, my age is something I have shared voluntarily when creating my Account with Google maybe 10 years ago:

I provided my date of birth and gender which creating my account.

This is not surprising, but after scrolling down by interests I can see most of them are websites, I can remember visiting. Then I see that I am in the market for Financial and Accounting Software. When I click on it, I realise it is based on online activity while signed in on Google Search, YouTube and etc.

After my boyfriend watched some finance videos on YouTube on my browser, I am now in the market for Financial Software.

With one click this can be turned off if you believe that any of these are not relevant to you anymore. As you go through the list, you will easily recognise the Affinity Categories and In-Market Segments you have been put in.

If you click on *Manage your activity* from any of the explanation cards you will be able to see what websites you have seen and all other activity on Google's platforms.

It's fascinating to see the daily activity which you would otherwise not remember. For me one of the biggest surprises was the amount of Google searches I have done on average per day. I hardly remembered doing any of them. When seeing them individually, I would recognise the activity, but if you asked me what websites I visited yesterday, I would hardly remember.

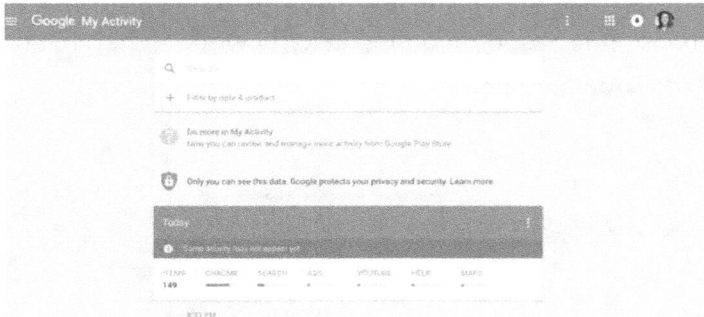

The use of smart mobile devices with internet access has made the fusion between online and offline activity so smooth that we do not even feel it. So many of these searches, YouTube video watches have happened on the go, while walking to work or shopping in a store.

This is a great way to understand how Google collects information and what you can expect from targeting Affinity Categories, In-Market segments and their Custom versions. It can be very powerful, but you cannot avoid some inaccuracy. In the case of my detected interest in Financial and Accounting Software, I realised this was because of a YouTube video a friend of mine watched on my laptop while I was away.

Remarketing and Similar Audience

The last option from the Audience section of your campaign builder is Remarketing and Similar Audience. You might have heard of Remarketing as it is becoming common topic, but there is not much information available of how to do it and a lot of people are confusing it with all other Display targeting.

So what is Remarketing?

Remarketing(or remarketing) is a way of targeting people who have already been on your website or have shared their personal data and given you permission to use it for marketing purposes.

When it comes to Remarketing of web visitors the process involves collecting cookies on your website. You might have seen messages warning you that a certain website uses cookies and you must accept it. Then you wondered what does that even mean.

A cookie is a long string of numbers which your website attaches to a web visitor's browser to identify this user. I would like to make it clear a – the user's identity stays completely anonymous. All the data that you have collected is their IP(Internet Protocol) address, the time of the visit, the duration, pages viewed, videos watched, button clicked, etc. From this information it is impossible to find out the user's identity. This is legal and is not breaching your web visitors' privacy as long as the little message that you are using cookies is present on your website.

Your browser has probably a lot of cookies stored already if you have not cleaned them recently. To see your cookies in Google Chrome, just open an empty tab and go to the three vertical dots in the top right corner and choose Settings.

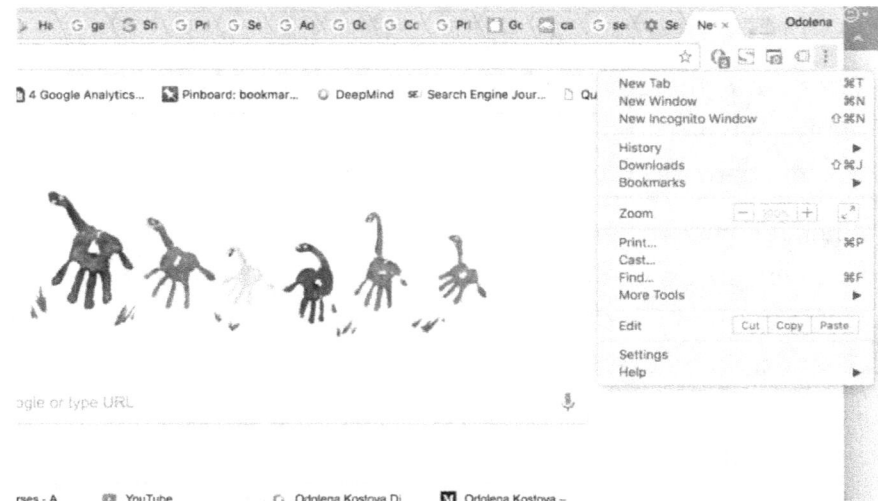

Then scroll down to Advanced and Choose Content Settings. Here you can control what websites can and cannot access when you visit them. The first option is Cookies, but then you have also things like Location, Microphone, Camera and Notifications. If you choose these to be blocked, you will keep getting messages from websites asking if you could share this information. You can then choose when this is necessary and when you prefer to stay anonymous.

If you select Cookies and then See All Cookies Data, you will see a spectacular history of websites which have tracked your activity and might have you in their remarketing lists. This might explain the ads you are seeing. You can click on any of them and see the name of the website and when you have visited it. You can easily delete your cookie data if you want to free some space. Cookie data is collected in different folders on your computer, depending on the browser you are using. For Google Chrome it is here:

C:\Users\your_username\AppData\Local\Google\Chrome\User Data\Default\

How to start collecting cookies from your web visitors?

THE ULTIMATE ONLINE MARKETING GUIDE

If you want to remarket your web visitors based on cookies, you must allow access to Google to collaborate. There are two ways to do this – through Google AdWords or through Google Analytics. I would advise you to create a Google Analytics account, as you will need to analyse how people interact with your website anyway. I will not go in much detail in this process, because Google Analytics is not the main topic of this book and also setting it up varies depending on how your website is built. But these are the basics:

To create a Google Analytics account go to analytics.google.com and get started with the setup. There are two levels in an Account. The first one is Properties and Apps – these are the different websites and applications you own and would like to track. For each of them you can have different Views – i.e. All Website Data, Data from certain part of the website, etc.

This is how your home page looks like once you have created the account:

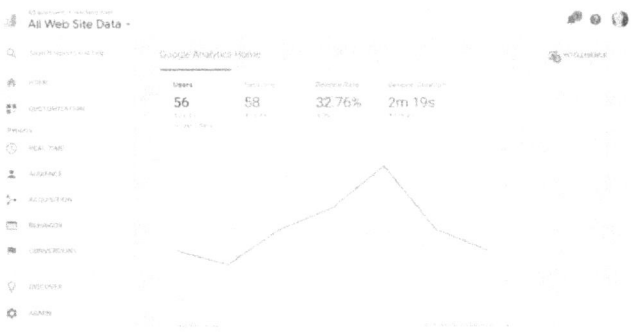

Before installing Google Analytics on your website, you will not see any data displayed. To make the installation go to Admin - the last tab on the left. Then choose Tracking info and then Tracking code:

Your tracking code will be displayed in a window. This code must be added in the footer of all the pages of your website. If you are using a WordPress website, you can easily do this by installing a plug-in and adding the code to the plug-in. You can then test by sending test traffic to see if it worked out.

To enable Analytics to collect Remarketing data, just go to data Collection(under Tracking Code). Then the only thing you have checked is that Remarketing is enabled.

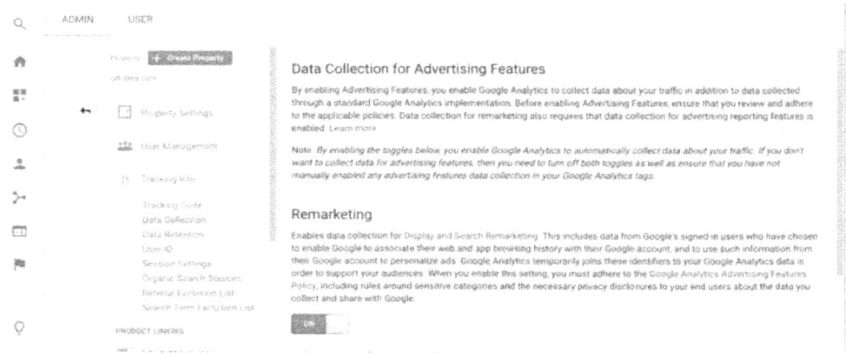

Then you must connect your Analytics account to your Google AdWords. You must first enable your AdWords account to connect with Analytics. To do this click on the wrench icon in the top right corner and select Linked Accounts under Setup.

THE ULTIMATE ONLINE MARKETING GUIDE

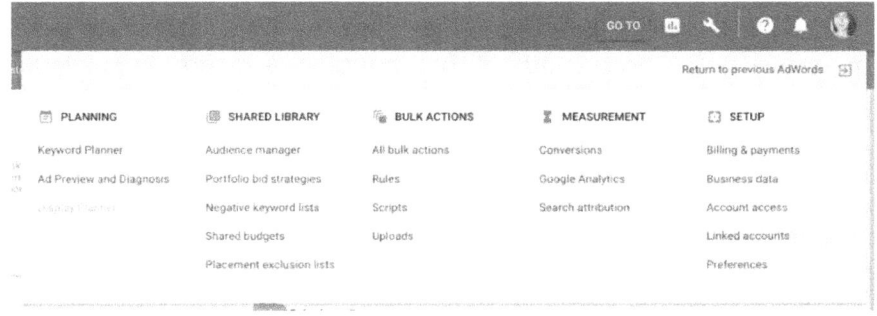

The simply select Google Analytics and enter the email associated with your Google Analytics account. This is it – now you can share information between the two accounts.

Creating an audience in Google Analytics

First log in Google Analytics and click on Admin. In the Property row select Audiences Definitions and then Audiences.

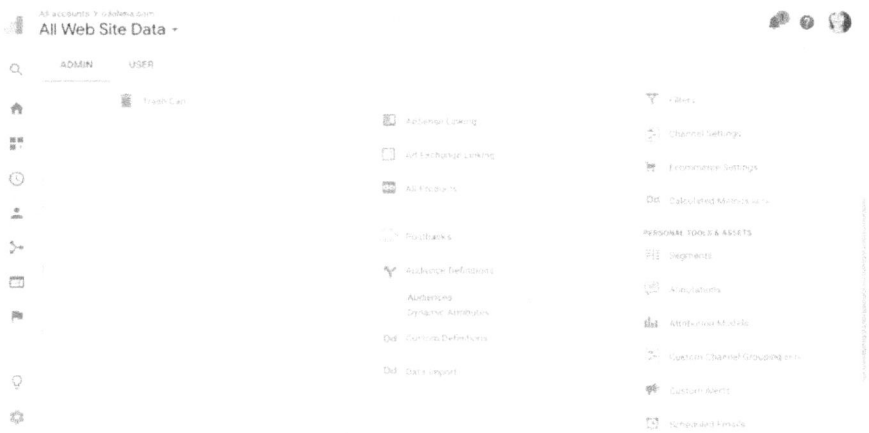

You will see a red button saying New Audience. By clicking on it, you open the Google Analytics audience builder. Here you have a lot of opportunities for remarketing and other targeting options.

There is an option to choose to target people who already converted, new or returning visitors, people who visited a particular section of your website. If you choose Create New, you can also select also other options.

1. **Demographics**

This section contains demographic data like age, location, gender, as well as In-Market Segments and Affinity Categories. You can easily put this filter on if you would like to remarket only certain type of web visitors.

2. **Behaviour**

Here you can choose to target users by the actions they took on your website like session duration, number of sessions, days after the last session, number of transactions.

3. **Date of First Session**

You can choose to filter out visitors who visited your website before a certain date, especially if you changed the function of the website in the meantime.

4. **Traffic Sources**

Here you can determine a group of web visitors by the source they are coming from. If you are running a campaign on Facebook, you might want to have users who came through it to have a different journey after.

5. **Conditions**

This is the option you will probably use most often. Here you can define a URL which users have visited as a rule for your audience. For example, if you would like to remarket people who are interested in a particular product, you can choose the page featuring this product as a definition. This is great if you would like to show consistent tailored advertising to your visitors.

6. Sequences

Here you can target users who have seen certain parts of your website in a particular order. For example, people who have come to your website from a particular ad and then downloaded a brochure. Then, you could retarget them with an ad to encourage them to take another action.

Once you set up your audience requirements, you can set up the membership duration. The longer the period, the larger audience you're going to retarget. However you might end up showing ads to people who already bought from you. To eliminate this, you can set up a condition to exclude the visitors of a page which is accessible only after a purchase.

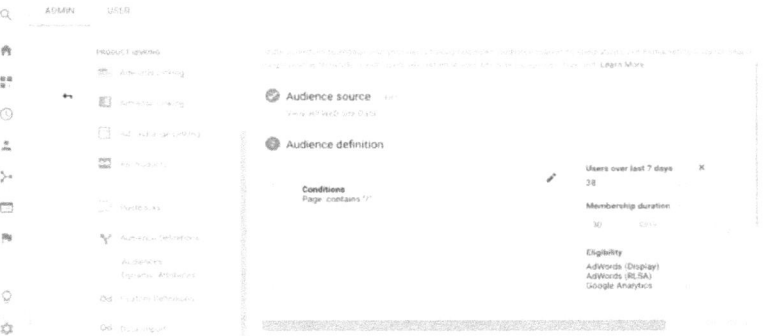

You will get an estimation of the number of users on your list for the last 7 days. This can give you an idea about the potential size of your audience. Also you will see for which purposes you can use your audience. Remarketing lists based on cookies are eligible to show ads on Google Search(RLSA) and Display Network, as well as be used for analysis in Google Analytics.

If you are asking yourself, what is a good-sized audience, it really depends on the size of your market and type of product you are trying to push. If an audience is too small you are not likely to get any results; if it is too large, you might end up showing to irrelevant people. This is why I would suggest choosing an audience which is not smaller than 2000 users to get any results.

Depending on your budget, scale and website traffic, the upper barrier can be very high. Still, remember that users online expect a personalised experience. Segmenting your lists by web pages, actions completed and excluding certain users, can help you achieve better results with your remarketing efforts.

To finalise the audience creation, choose the Google AdWords account you would like to send the audience to. When you log in Google AdWords you will be able to access the new audience and add it to your campaign. If you are managing more than one account in an MCC(My Client Centre), you can easily share audiences between the different accounts in AdWords.

Similar Audiences

Once you have created a remarketing audience via Google Analytics, it will automatically be imported into your linked AdWords account. Then is a matter of a few days for Google to create a similar audience out of your remarketing list. A similar audience is a list of users who have close interests, demographics and behaviour to your audience. These are entirely new people, who might have never heard of your brand. The remarketing list is used in this case only as a source for Google to set up criteria for a similar audience.

The size of a similar audience can be much larger than a remarketing list. A well-defined smaller remarketing list is likely to provide you with a big and relevant similar audience. The reason is that it is easier for Google to find common interests and other similarities in a smaller group than a larger one.

The diagram above shows how Google creates similar audiences from Customer lists. You can see how users from similar audiences can outnumber the initial source. All customer data which is not matched to registered Google Accounts is then deleted.

If you think of all your website users, it would be clear to you that they all have different goals to be on your website. Creating an audience which is similar to all of your users, is likely to result in very broad criteria and a lot of users who have a vague similarity to the people you are after.

Remember, similar audiences are not remarketing. They are based on existing website visitors lists or customer email uploads, but they are *new* to your brand. When choosing your message think of them as a completely new audience which is likely to be interested in what you offer.

Not all similar audiences can be used on all Google Display Platforms. Customer email uploads can only be used to target users on Gmail, YouTube or Google Shopping and same for similar audiences created from email uploads. These platforms require users to log in with their email accounts, whereas third-party websites using AdSense don't.

Other display targeting

Let's return to the Display Campaign Builder. After you have chosen any Affinity Categories, In-Market Segments, Remarketing, or Similar audiences, there is another opportunity to add a demographic filter.

Demographic targeting

Here you still have the opportunity to target by parent status. I say still because as I am writing this book targeting by income became unavailable for the United Kingdom. This income data is available through a partnership between Google and official sources like The U.S. Census Bureau for example. This option is available only for certain countries which at the moment when I am writing the book are Australia, Brazil, Hong Kong, India, Indonesia, Japan, Mexico, New Zealand, South Korea, Singapore, Thailand and the U.S.

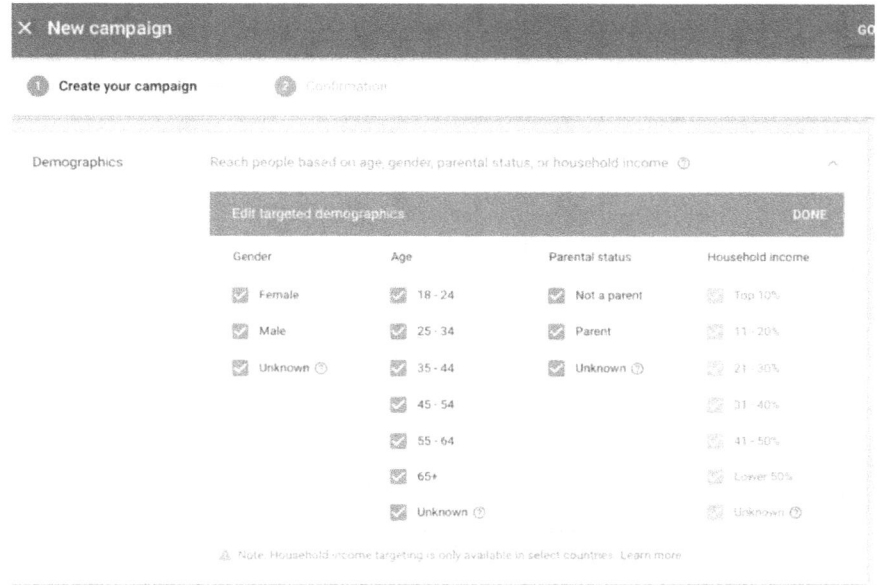

While I was writing this book the income targeting became unavailable in the United Kingdom.

I would recommend you to keep unknown in all categories as you might be restricting a lot of visitors who preferred not to share their demographic data, but they still can be very useful to you, especially if you are doing remarketing.

Content targeting

Here you can add some display keywords. As we mentioned before display keywords are slightly different from search keywords – they are more contextual rather than direct query related. If you have already created a Custom Intent audience based on keywords, you can skip this section.

If you would like to add display keywords, simply type in a keyword or a website address to start getting ideas. The only important part is to choose if you would like to target by Content or Audience at the bottom of the display keyword planner. I would always go for the Audience type of targeting because I would like to show ads to people even if they are browsing unrelated topics. As long as you have ticked on some content exclusions to keep your ads out of sensitive content, this is the better option.

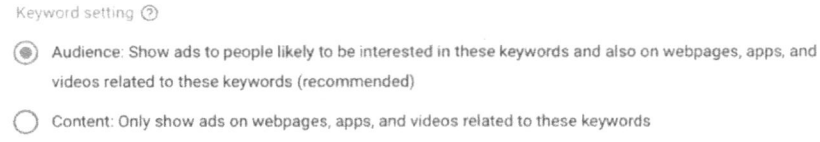

You can also choose placement which can be certain websites where you would like to show your ads on. You can also select YouTube channels, YouTube Videos, Apps and App Categories from Google Play or Apple App Store. Obviously, the Campaign Builder is suited for all kinds of Google Campaigns, but in our case, we are creating a Display Campaign with banner ads. The only choice which makes sense is websites.

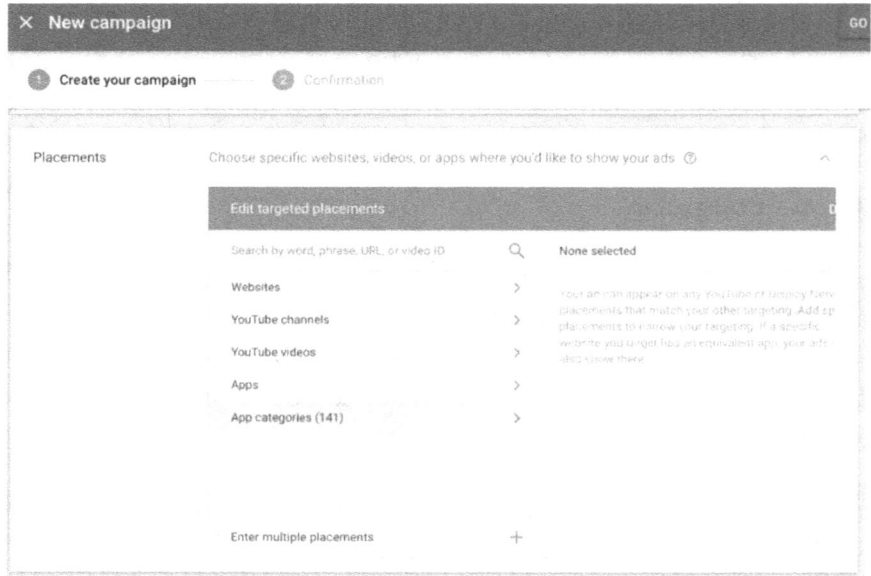

You can also choose topics, which are very similar to the In-Market Segments we talked about. If you are doing remarketing, I would not recommend you to decrease the size of your audience by adding too many filters. The fact that they have visited a page of your website is already a strong interest signal for you.

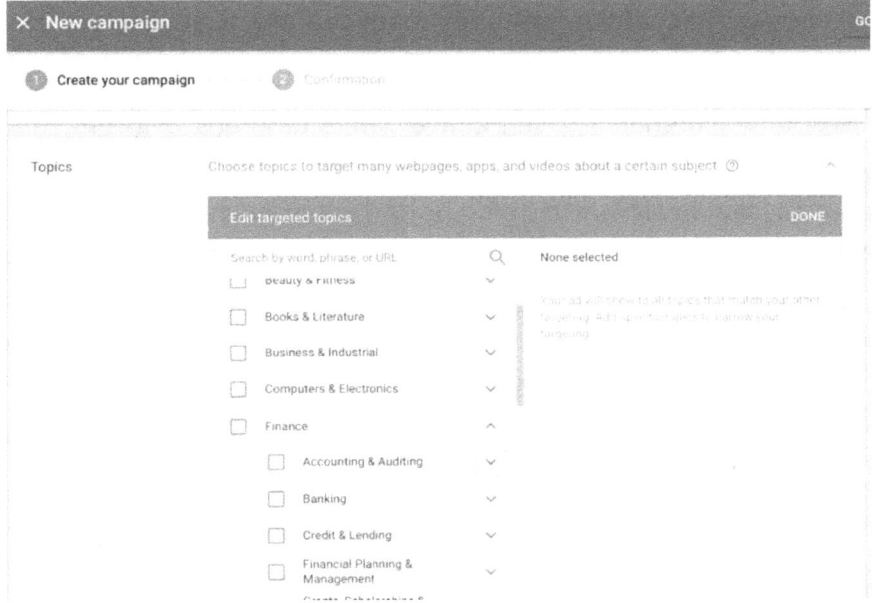

Automated Targeting

The last Display Campaign Setting is called Automated Targeting. This allows Google to expand the audience you have already defined in the previous steps. This is a way of showing to more people if you cannot reach them with other targeting options.

Conservative targeting is available to all Display campaigns and does not require any historic conversion data. A way of using Conservative Targeting is by adding it to the remarketing list you have created already. If you are targeting users who viewed a page of your website about excursions to Cambodia, Google will then try to find more people interested in this destination, based on their online behaviours.

Aggressive targeting requires at least 15 conversions recorded the last 30 days in this campaign to function. It will try to get you as many conversions as possible. However, this setting can increase your cost per conversion and is not recommended for advertisers with a limited budget.

From my experience, even Conservative targeting might increase your cost per conversion, but it will definitely help you reach more people. I would always try to do remarketing separately without any automated targeting to reach the people who have been already on my website with a personalised message. To expand my audience, I would take Custom Intent or a Similar audience and tweak the ad copy to be suitable for new visitors.

Creating Responsive Display Ads

The next section of your campaign creation is making display ads. Until recently, banner ads could only be created outside of Google AdWords and be imported in the platform. If you have already ads done for you by a designer or you make your own ads using Photoshop, that's great.

If you are about to create your display ads from scratch there are a few things to have in mind.

1. Always include your logo. Google will disapprove ads without a logo.
2. Use standard sizes with are approved by Google and can be displayed on the majority of the display network. You can find all the acceptable sizes on Google's support page.

3. Include a call to action button on your ad, relevant to your landing page. If your landing page is a sales page, the CTA must be something like "Buy Now". If your landing page is an information page, the button should say "Learn More".

Google made it really easy for advertisers to create display ads without having to use any professional design support or even without leaving the Google AdWords platform.

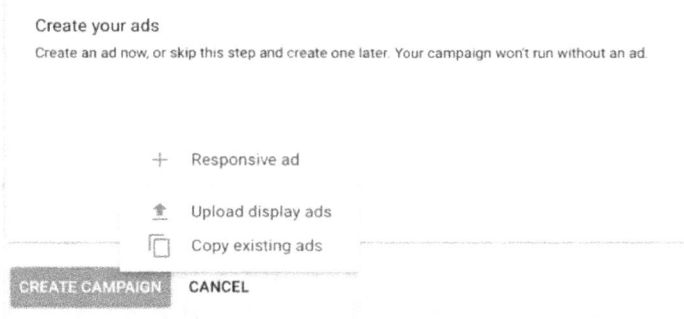

In your campaign builder, when "Create Ad", you can either upload the ads you have already or create something called a Responsive ad. Responsive ads are a new type which basically requires just a logo, a few images and a couple of lines of text. Google automatically shapes and sizes them into banners in about 8 million variations. The Responsive ads appear in all shapes and sizes and fit in all the placements available. This helps you get maximum chance of visibility, but you have zero control on how ads can look like.

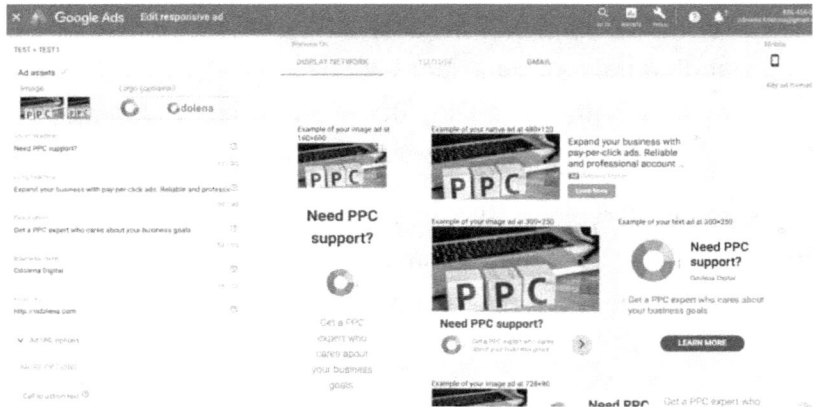

To get started choose images and you will see Google is automatically scanning the website you have provided looking for images. So now This is great to get your logo immediately uploaded. You must have 2 logos - one square and one rectangle. For main images it is generally recommended to pick around 15 variations, which Google can test with the different ads sizes. You can use your website scanned images; you can upload or get stock images.

When you click "Save", you will see a preview of your ads.

Then enter one short and one long headline, a description and your business name. You can edit your CTA button and choose a different language. Click add to ad group and you are ready. I would advise you to create as many variations as possible, so Google can test with them and pick the best performing one.

Finalising your campaign

Once you have created your ad group, you can choose if you want to use automated targeting. You can choose from no automation, conservative automation, aggressive automation. Automatic targeting helps optimise your targeting across the Display Network, letting you reach people your targeting wouldn't otherwise reach, at around the same cost per person automatically. If you want to do purely remarketing, I would not recommend any automation, because this might expand your audience also to some similar audiences.

If your remarketing list is for people visiting travel sites about Japan, conservative targeting may extend to people visiting sites about Tokyo tourist destinations. Aggressive targeting might go further if the data supports it—it can expand independently of manual targeting based on predicted conversions.

Ad group bid – choose how much you would like to bid for a click or viewable impressing depending on your setting. You normally get an estimation from Google of how much you should bid benchmarked to advertisers with similar targeting.

And now you are ready to create your display campaign.

19. ADVERTISING ON YOUTUBE

YouTube became part of Google in 2006, only about a year it was founded. Since then Google has been looking for ways to monetise the channel with video ads. In the last year the efforts have been going in the direction to turn YouTube into a platform for conversions.

So far, YouTube has been traditionally understood as a platform for brand top-of-the-funnel types of campaigns. Marketers focusing on conversions like sign ups, sales, app installs were focusing on other channels to achieve their goals. The truth is that it used to be very hard to track direct ROI form YouTube be ads and to attribute conversions to a video watch. Now technology is changing and YouTube is turning gradually into a more performance driven platform.

YouTube has a lot of benefits to offer advertisers on every stage of the funnel. There is an abundance of targeting options based on how users interacted with your brand, their interests and previous YouTube and Google Search history. Ad formats like True View can help you reach audiences, without being intrusive. In this chapter I will explain which features apply for you according to your goals.

Why should you consider YouTube?

There are 5 billion YouTube videos watched on average daily.

Over 60% of the sessions on YouTube are on mobile and an average session on mobile lasts 40 minutes.

YouTube videos are significantly related to purchasing behaviour. It is not only cute cats that people watch but also, they use video content to find out about all kinds of products – from food, to vacations, to cars and services. The wide spectrum of content available on the platform is astonishing.

As of July 2015, more than 400 hours of video were uploaded to YouTube every minute, up from 300 hours per minute in November 2014.

YouTube Ad Formats

True View In-Stream

One of the best products for marketers on YouTube is the True View In-Stream ad. This is the skippable format which can appear before, in the middle or after a video. The advertiser is charged only when a user decides not to skip the ad. They must watch more than 30 seconds or interact with the video by clicking, liking, commenting or sharing – whichever comes first. This shows a strong interest in the content and only then you must pay.

Another great feature of this format is the opportunity to create remarketing lists from the users who have already clicked on the ad. In this way you can create a real journey for your prospect by showing them a different creative in every remarketing list.

You can add a call to action button overlay on your video which would encourage the user to convert. The call to action must be very clear and understandable. A click on the call to action can lead the user either to a landing page or to the channel itself. An ad can be used to either grow a channel or for any other type of conversion like a sale, sign up, app install.

The True View In-Stream may appears together with a companion banner on the right side. This is similar to the banner ad which appear on the display network, but it only appears next to a video ad, making it even more prominent on the feed. When clicking on the banner users are redirected to a landing page.

You can technically create a banner ad display campaign targeting only YouTube as a placement without videos. However, these ads can only use the Google Display Campaign targeting, not the Video Campaign targeting. This means you cannot target a YouTube channel or video, use customer lists audience or retarget your YouTube Channel subscribers.

True View for Action

As Google evolves more and more into a performance marketing platform, there are new options for driving action. With True View In-Stream you can add action button under the video. This subtype is called True View for Action. The button will lead the user to a landing page where they can complete the action you called out – sign up with a form, download a document, etc.

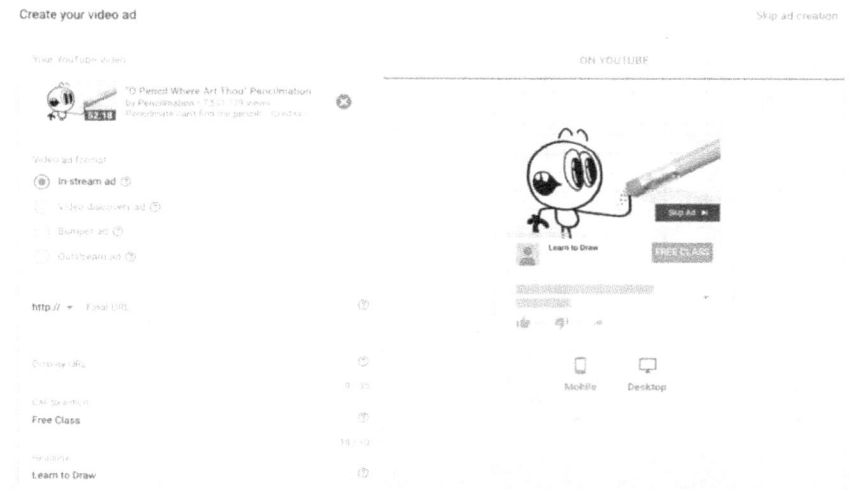

You can finally enhance the experience by creating cards which lead the user to a next video they can watch. You can see a creative example of Lego who did a scenario type of ad. The story has three possible ends and you can choose which one is the "right" one by watching the next video. This increases engagement which the brand, time spend on the channel, but not the cost of the ad.

Also you can create product cards, connected to your Google Merchant Centre to display certain products as expandable cards along the video and redirect customers to buy them. This is the beginning of a very exciting period for YouTube as the platform is redesigned to make it easier for advertisers to achieve their goals like sign ups, purchases and app installs.

True View Discovery ads

This is as close as you can get to a "Sponsored post" type of ad on YouTube. These ads will appear on top of YouTube(including the YouTube mobile app) search and watch pages, as well as publisher sites and apps across the Google Display Network.

With this YouTube ad you are charged only when a user clicks on your ad and watches your video. From the name of the ad you get the feeling that this format is meant to be for expanding your brand awareness. It encourages users to see new content which otherwise will difficultly reach out to them organically.

True View for Mobile App Installs

This format appears as a Call-to-Action banner under a video ad with a button redirecting to Google Play or the App Store. The video can be showcasing how the application works and then users are offered the opportunity to download the app straight away. To create such campaign you must choose Universal App Install campaign type, not Video Campaign.

Then with Universal App Install you can decide which property of Google to target – Search, Display, YouTube or the Play Store.

You can set up the campaign to optimise for the volume of app installs or for in app actions. Google's and Ipsos' recent study shows that a quarter of installed apps never get used. This brings up the question of whether app installs volume is a good metric to track. In order to optimise for app install actions, you must have conversion tracking installed.

All True View ads count to the number of the YouTube video which you are using for an ad creative if they have been watched longer than 11 seconds.

Bumper ads

Bumper ads are a short video format which cannot be skipped. It plays before, during or after a video and has a 6-second duration. This is a great format for brand awareness and reach. The bumper ads have no call to action button; they are just quick video messages to create awareness.

Bumper ads can appear on YouTube, Google partner video sites and apps on the Display Network. You will be charged by thousand impressions (CPM), regardless if they are all counted as "viewable" or not.

Outstream Campaigns

These are video campaigns designed for increasing brand awareness outside of YouTube – on Google video partner sites for mobile and tablet devices on apps and mobile websites.

To create an Outstream campaign, you can start like usually with the + button in the Campaigns Section of Google AdWords and select a Video campaign as a type. Then you must choose as a goal Brand

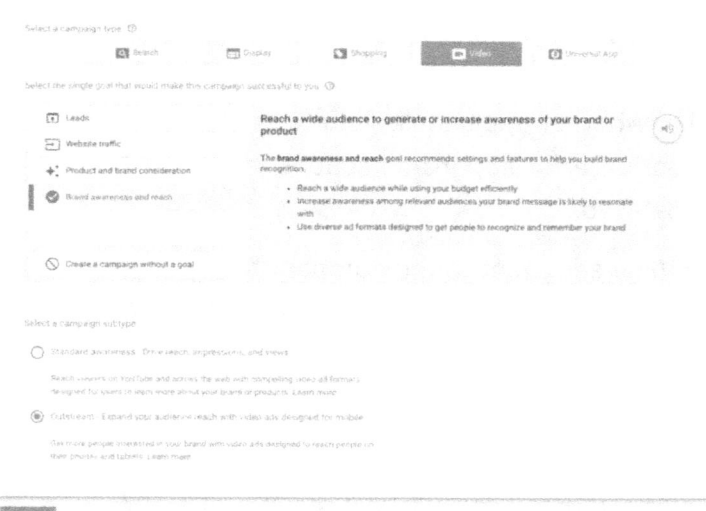

Awareness and Reach. You will then see two choices under the setup – a Standard campaign and an Outstream campaign.

The ads are really easy to create – you only need a video, logo, headline, business name and two description lines. These campaigns are mobile-only, so they are a great way to reach more users, as many users block ads on desktop. You are charged only per viewable CPM – when you reach a 1000 impressions. An impression is counted as viewable only if more than 50% of the ad was seen in the screen fold and was exposed to the user for longer than 2 seconds.

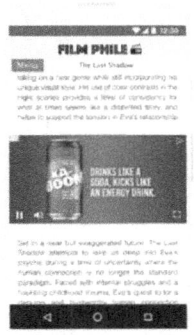

Lightbox ads

These ads responsively combine your ad assets – like videos, image galleries and maps – to fill available ad spaces. Lightbox ads may contain multiple videos, image galleries or combinations of these

To create a lightbox ad, you must start by creating a Display campaign, not Video campaign and choose Brand Awareness and Consideration as an objective. Then Lightbox format will automatically be available in your campaign builder.

You can choose images, videos by scanning your website, searching on YouTube or just uploading them. If you use Google Shopping (Google's product ads for e-commerce, which is a topic of a whole new book), you can upload cards with your products which can appear on the side of the video. You can add a call to action, links to your landing pages and a cover image for your video. The final result is something like this:

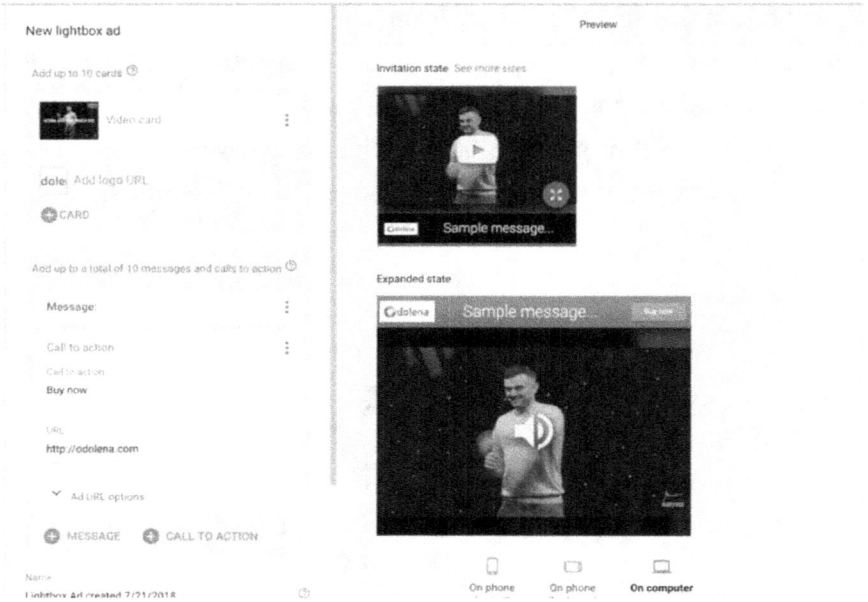

When people engage with Lightbox ads by clicking, tapping or hovering, the ads respond. Lightbox ads may expand to fill the screen, display videos or allow people to tap through a set of images, eventually coming to your website. The closest equivalent of Lightbox ads is the Canvas ad on Facebook.

Lightbox ads are available at vCPM (cost per thousand viewable impressions) or (Cost per Engagement). In the new interface only the second option is available. If the ad is already expanded, a "user engagement" means that the user hovers, clicks or taps to expand the ad and the ad has time to load and be seen. If the ad is not expanded yet, then an engagement is when the user interacts with it after is it displays.

If you still cannot picture what a Lightbox ad is in reality, think of the small videos pinned up in the corner of a blog article which follow you while scrolling down. This is one example of a rich and interactive format, but it helps to differentiate it from the standard YouTube video ads.

Reserved Media Placements on YouTube

If your business or agency is planning a big rebranding or new product awareness campaign you can reach directly to a Google Representative and reserve ads on YouTube. With this option you have access to an agreed amount of impressions at a certain placement on a fixed price. This gives more control and also allows you to choose from ad formats which are not available through Google AdWords.

There are two options to be charged – Cost per thousand impressions(CPM), where the cost is agreed in advance or cost per day(CPD) for certain formats. Campaigns done through Reserved Media Placements on YouTube must be booked in advance – 9 or 6 days depending on the campaign. The creative must be sent to Google also in advance, as you cannot build these campaigns through AdWords.

Ad formats which are available are:

- Standard In-Stream. These are non-skippable 15 to 30-second ads which appear before a video. You rarely see these now and now you know why – they have to be booked in advance and cannot be created by every advertiser.

- In-Stream Select. These are skippable ads, similar to True View In-Stream, but in this case they only play at the beginning of the video, never during or after. They can be only up to 60 seconds long, not like True View In-stream which has no limit.

The examples above are available as a CPM payment and have a strict video format. There are also other formats which can only be booked at a cost per day price (CPD).

- Desktop Custom Masthead. This is a 950 X 270 unit seen on top of the YouTube homepage on desktop devices. This can be still or a video format. Often you will see Google products' ads there and most often a very famous company.
- Desktop Universal Video Masthead. This is a 780 x 195 that runs on the YouTube homepage. It includes a video on one side and an information panel or a flash/image panel on the other. The flash/image panel can optionally expand/close when someone clicks on/closes it.
- Mobile Video Masthead. This is the ad you see on top of the YouTube app homepage. It is a video format, which also has a CTA button. The video is still on mobile, whereas on desktop it is on without sounds.

Here is an example of a Converse shoes campaign which I spotted on YouTube, using the Mastheads format on all devices:

On desktop:

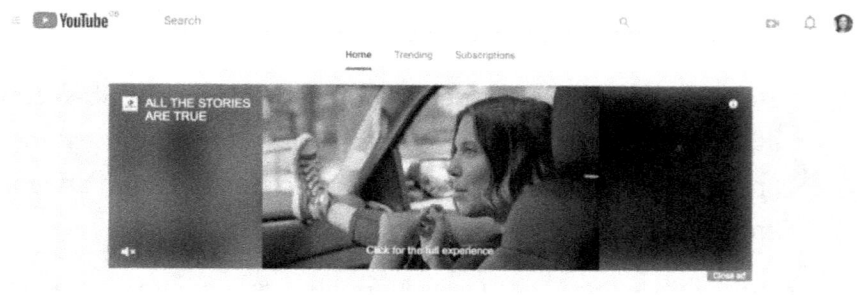

...and on mobile:

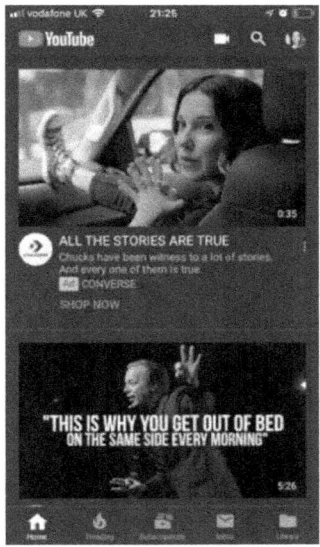

As you might imagine such campaigns are expensive. Actually the cost is between $300-400,000 per day and even higher on a significant day like a seasonal holiday or a sports event and of course the targeting option.

However they can be extremely effective to create massive awareness about a product. Compared to TV ads cost – still a bargain! I just felt I must explain how they work, as they are part of the YouTube advertising ecosystem and coexist with Google AdWords-built ads.

There are a few upcoming ad formats which at the time of the writing of this book(July 2018) were just announced, but not yet fully available for advertisers. These are not entirely YouTube ads, but they live on all Google Properties – Search, Display, Google Maps and YouTube.

Local Campaigns

To businesses which focus only on getting people in store like restaurants or car dealerships, Google announced a new type of campaigns called Local Campaigns. These allow businesses to advertise across all Google's properties with a single campaign. They must have a Google My Business account (they must list their business on Google Maps) and a linked YouTube account, as well as a few images and text. The campaigns have automated targeting and bidding based on the budget, the product and the goal of the campaign, similar to the Smart Display Campaigns.

Smart Shopping Campaigns

Smart Shopping Campaigns are e-commerce campaigns which allow advertisers to show ads across search, YouTube, Display and Google Maps with the same campaign. The targeting and bidding are automated and based on the product feed data and past conversion history. To be able to run Smart Shopping Campaign you need minimum 20 conversions in the last 30 days and a linked to AdWords Google My Business and YouTube accounts.

What's even better is that no product feed is needed to be uploaded. Google Shopping campaigns will be able to scan the website and get automated product feeds. This will be launched later in 2018.

Smart Shopping campaigns come with new goals besides Maximize Clicks, Target ROAS and Maximize Conversion Value. The goals will be focused on getting new customers and increasing in-store visits. This is great for businesses which would like to sell both on and offline.

YouTube Marketing Metrics

There are a few things to think about when assessing the performance of your YouTube video campaign.

Average cost per view(CPV)

To calculate this, you can divide the total cost of all ad views by the number of views your ad received. A view is counted when a video ad is watched more than 30 seconds.

The average CPV is different from your maximum CPV in the same way as your average CPC is different from your max CPC on Google Search or Display. What you will pay for a view depends on the ad length, the quality of the creative, the targeting and auction dynamics. A raising CPV might mean an increasing competition. The more restricted your targeting is, the higher the competition and the higher the CPV. If you have more broad targeting, the ad-serving system can identify auctions in which your ad is more competitive.

To relax campaign restrictions, make sure your delivery method is not Accelerated, let your ad rotation to optimise for best performing ads and rethink your platform targeting. Also adjust your bids, having in mind the real value of your ad being played. Have in mind you have owned, paid and earned views. Owned views are organic views of the video you use for an ad creative. Paid are the ones you pay for with your campaign. You earn views if your video ad is shared, so in this case you have paid one view, but received much more. Lastly, you can improve your ad creative, as high-quality creatives get a better CPV.

View Rate (VR)

The view rate is the ratio between the total number of ad views divided by the total number of impressions. In YouTube impressions are the times when your ad has been displayed. If this is a True View

In-Stream ad impression is the time when your ad started to play, regardless if it was skipped or not. If it is a True View Discovery ad every time your video thumbnail appeared in the YouTube search or in partner websites or apps.

To improve your view rate, you can test a shorter ad creative. Also rethink your video and try to tell a story to make it more compelling. Make sure you have several ads rotating to avoid "ad fatigue" and see which one performs better.

Click-through rate (CTR)

This is the ration between clicks and impressions and is valid for all ad formats. You can measure CTR as the level of engagement with your video ad. To increase CTR you can include product cards or cards with other videos, call to action overlays or a companion banner. You can also review your ad placements and exclude placements with a low CTR.

YouTube over delivery

Sometimes when YouTube's ad-serving system detects high volume of good traffic it can automatically spend up to 2 times more of your daily budget. It will then even this out over the next days by underspending. After one month your total spend will always be your daily budget multiplied by 30.4.

YouTube Analytics

In this book, I did not get deeply in analytics tools, as this is a huge topic. I will explain how to use some of the free reports on YouTube Analytics to understand your ads' performance and optimise it.

THE ULTIMATE ONLINE MARKETING GUIDE

With your YouTube channel you get a fee YouTube Analytics platform to track the performance of both, your organic and paid video campaigns. To access it got to your channel, click Video Manager.

Then select Analytics from the left side menu lane.

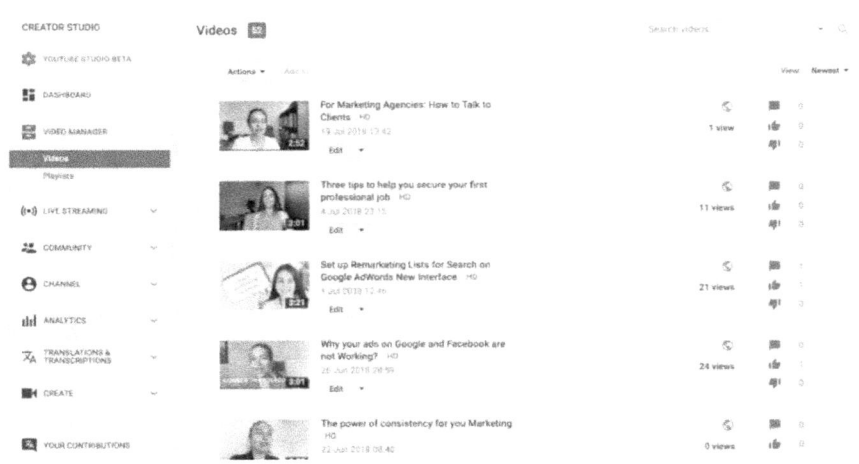

There are two reports you must pay attention to:

Audience Retention Report

Here you can check the average view duration of all videos, including the ones you use for ads. It outlines your top videos or channels by watch time. Also, you can see what is the average percentage watched of your video. If you check relative audience retention, you can see how your video compares to other similar videos on YouTube for audience retention. If this video is used for an ad there will be two graphs – one for paid and one for organic.

Interaction reports

Here you can track the engagement with your video – comments, shares and likes. If you are using cards and CTA overlays you can track their performance here. Also, you can get an understanding of your subscribers – whether you are gaining or losing any after every video you have shared.

Make the Ultimate True View Video Creative

The video creative you use is one of the most important parts of the success of your video campaign. There are differences between a successful organic video and a successful video ad.

Start with a smile

First, if you are running an In-Stream skippable ad, you are interrupting the experience of a user who is trying to play another video. You must justify the interruption with an excellent quality ad which is relevant to them and you must do this in 5 seconds, after which they can skip. Studies of Google show that a smiling face, watching in the camera is the best way to start a video ad. Also talking directly to the camera makes a better connection with the user. Make sure you have the camera a on eye level, never below or above. In this way you act as a peer, neither superior or inferior to the viewer.

Introduce the brand immediately

The brand must be also almost instantly visible and audible. It is preferable to have your logo seen and your brand name said at the same time. This reassures the viewer what the ad is about and whether it is relevant for them or not. Tricking people to watch your ad only to realise this is not something they are interested can give you the false impression you are doing good with a high View Rate. However this View Rate might not translate in taking any action down the funnel. Remember, with True View In-Stream you pay for each viewer who watched 30 seconds of your ad or interacted with it – whichever comes first.

Tell them what to do next

Using a Call to Action in the video is also crucial. The more precise the CTA, the better. You must explain to the visitor exactly what the next step should be – where they can click to see more information or purchase the product if you want them to download an app or sign up on a form. Using a CTA overlay can help you have a link to your landing page appearing on top of the video as text on a transparent background.

After 30 seconds they are yours

Your ad can be as long as you wish after the minimum 30 seconds. At this point you have achieved your goal – not only they did not skip, they stayed for another 25 seconds with you. They are clearly interested!

Actually, having along video might be a great way to segment your audience by the length of watch. There are brands which have an hour-long video as a True View In-Stream ad and surprisingly they see some users watching all of it.

One example is the clothing brand Gant. They knew their buyers were an intelligent and curious group – people who tend to watch interviews on YouTube on subjects like science, technology and entrepreneurship.

They created a series of interviews by the celebrity couple, comedian Craig Ferguson and his wife speaking to some prominent people from technology, science and business. The interviews played as True View In-Stream video ads and lasted about half an hour. The only way the brand was shown was that the speakers were wearing it. Guest speakers included people like Kimbal Musk (the brother of Elon Musk) and Neil deGrasse Tyson.

Gant achieved an incredible view rate of 71% on a 35% cheaper CPV due to their extremely high-quality ads and engaging content. On Facebook and Instagram they used shorter videos of 30 seconds with an even cheaper cost per view.[7]

Use Personalities

The example above includes another winning strategy on YouTube – using influencers and famous personalities. You might not have to world-known comedians and entrepreneurs to get your ad View Rate up, but consider collaborating with influencers in your field. Like Gant did, make sure you carefully research your audience and what matters to them, before coming up with a concept for your video.

Humour

Entertainment is a big part of the reason why people are on YouTube. Your ad might be interrupting funny video users are watching, so make sure you keep them entertained. A lot of successful YouTube ads involve comedians(Gant's ad, too) and funny personalities. Even if this is not your case, you can still come up with a funny animation character or tell a story with humour.

Music

When it comes to music tests of YouTube do not show whether there is relationship between using music in the video and getting better performance. You can try this yourself considering also your placements – the channels and types of videos your ads will play on.

---

[7] https://www.precisdigital.com/case/massive-impact-youtube-serial-gant/

Animation

You can use animation to clarify what your product does. Animation videos are not very expensive to produce and can help you simplify a message. Users can find seeing a fun animated character as engaging as seeing a funny person or a celebrity.

Attractive Thumbnail

Thumbnails can increase organic and True View Discovery ad clicks. The thumbnail should clearly state why users should click on it and watch this video. Your title and video description also play a role when it comes to the click-through rate of the ad. The more descriptive and precise they are, the better. Users o YouTube are selective and often try to get to interesting and valuable information, so vague titles are not interesting.

Building Your YouTube Campaign

For every campaign objective, there is a YouTube solution you can use to reach prospects in every stage of the funnel. Before setting up a campaign think what the main objective of your campaign is.

Awareness

The homepage of YouTube has a prominent large placement on top. The ad you see there is called Masthead. Usually, the space is occupied by a large company; often it shows ads for Google itself. To get this placement you will have to contact a Google representative and pay a packaged fee for a certain period of time during which you would like your ad to be shown there.

A great option for an awareness campaign is an ad type called Bumper ad. This is a 6-second pre-roll ad which is not skippable and appears before a video plays. These ads can be set up directly through Google AdWords, no need to deal with a sales rep of Google.

You only need to upload your 6-second video on YouTube as a "Public" and create a campaign on Google AdWords.

Consideration

At this stage, you can use the two True View formats – the In-Stream which I mentioned above, as well as the Discovery ad. The last one is a type of ad which can appear in the search results of YouTube, partner websites and YouTube watch pages. It encourages users to watch the content as it looks like an organic video. You are only charged when someone clicks on the ad and watches the content.

At this stage remarketing and Google keywords is a great way to engage with an audience which you know is likely to consider your product. You can create a list of competitors names and target people who have recently searched for these brands. If you add also a remarketing list as an extra filter, i.e. you set the condition: they have been on my website and they are looking for competitors on Google, you get a very relevant audience. They are likely to have a strong buying intention and you seem to be one of their choices.

Driving action

Here come some of the newest solutions of YouTube which can really help performance marketers. We briefly mentioned the call to action overlay, but this is only one of the examples.

True View for Shopping is an ad type for an ecommerce. If you already have a Google Merchant Centre you can connect this one with your YouTube campaign by showing products from your feed below a video. For example, you are running a video ad showing a fashion collection. Below the ad you can have a stipe of products which are appearing in the video with a "Buy now" button and price.

True View for App Install is a great way to encourage more people to download your application. It is the same format – skippable after 5 seconds, but below the video there is a white line with a call to action button which links directly to Google Play or the App Store.

True View for Action can be used for any other type of conversion – sign up, download a form, subscribe for a newsletter, etc. In this case below the skippable video ad users will see a line promoting the product or service and a call to action button. This will take the user to a URL where they can take the action the advertiser is encouraging them to take. This is different from the call to action overlay. It is much more prominent and it has a clickable button, whereas the overlay is a small transparent ad which shows over the video.

Setting up your campaign is very easy in the new Google AdWords interface.

Step 1. Click the + button in the campaign section and choose Video campaign.

Step 2. Define the objective – website traffic, leads, product and brand consideration or brand awareness and reach. Depending on your choice there will be different types of types enabled in the campaign. For Outsream Campaigns and Bumper Ads choose Brand Awareness and Reach goal or no goal in the second case. To create True View Discovery ads and True View Shopping choose Product and brand consideration.

Step 3. – Define daily budget, start date and networks. In the case of a YouTube campaign placements can be specific channels, videos, as well as websites on the Display Network (only applicable to True

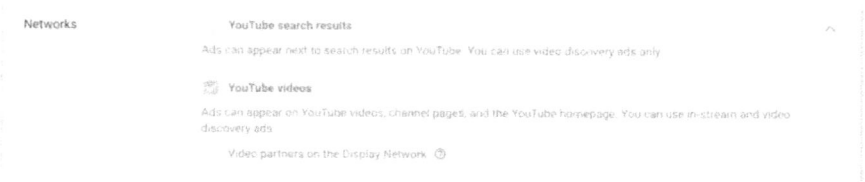

View Discovery ads). Depending on your campaign goal you will have some options greyed out and some ticked by default.

Continue with languages, locations and bidding strategy. Depending on the goal you have chosen you will have different strategies: Only Maximum CPV for Product and Brand Consideration, only Target CPA for Leads and Website Traffic, Maximum CPV or Maximum CPM for Brand awareness and reach and only Viewable CPM for Brand awareness and reach Outstream campaign. I know it is getting complicated, but just have in mind your objective and the recommended format for it – then just trust YouTube.

Step 4. Exclusions. Depending on how safe you would like to go with the exposure of your ad you can choose between Expanded, Standard and Limited inventory. Each of them contains differently classified YouTube video content. Remember, the more restrictions you choose, the higher CPV you can expect. You can also exclude videos on tragedy, conflict, sexually suggestive stuff, etc. as well as embedded, live streaming videos and games. There is also classification by labels like suitable for families, etc.

Make sure you set up a daily cap of your YouTube ad. The same way as with Display ads, you can restrict how many times a user can see an ad per day or week to assure you are not annoying people.

Step 5. Targeting. Here you can define who you would like to reach. You can select demographic filters and any of the audiences available for Google Display, plus customer uploaded lists and similar to customer lists. You can also retarget your YouTube channel subscribers or even people who watched one or more of your videos.

One unique option for targeting is called Life Events. This an audience based on upcoming important events detected by the online behaviour of the user – Marriage, Graduation, Moving. This is only available for YouTube and Gmail campaigns.

On top of this you can select keywords. These are different form the display keywords, which are more contextual, related to what websites users visit. In YouTube the keywords are related to the search queries on Google the users have done. This allows you to target people with a very specific buying intent. You can also add a filter of topics of interest, if you would like your ads to play on video content with a specific theme.

When selecting your targeting be careful not to make it too narrow, as your CPV will be higher. Make sure you understand the difference between Observation and Targeting setting. If you, for example, have a remarketing list of emails on Targeting and a list of keywords with the same setting, this means you only want to show your ads to people from the list who have searched for these keywords on Google while they are on YouTube. As you can imagine this is a very limited audience, which will not result in many opportunities for your ad to show.

Step 6. Placements. Depending on the goal you selected you will also have different placements available. For True View In-Stream ads you can target YouTube channels, partner video websites and apps on the GDN. You can also select on which videos and channels you would like your ad to play.

If making an Outstream campaign, you can select apps and mobile websites.

With True View Discovery ads you can only target YouTube website and the YouTube mobile app.

Step 7. Create your ad. Simply select the ad format you would like to have, search for the video you would like to use and select a landing page. If you are running a True View Discovery ad, you can direct users not only to a landing page, but to your own channel.

Press save and continue and you are ready!

YouTube Remarketing

Targeting options on YouTube are much more sophisticated than what is available on the other placements on the Google Display Network. You can use customer email lists, cookie based remarketing lists, interest and demography targeting.

One of the most interesting types of targeting is Custom Intent. This is basically keyword targeting. You can use contextual keywords, as well as Google search keywords. The second option gives you the opportunity to appear in front of people who have previously searched on Google for the keyword you are bidding on'

All forms of remarketing we talked about are available on YouTube – including customer match and some YouTube specific audiences like subscribers of your channel or users who interacted with your video content.

To be able to take advantage of the remarketing of YouTube audiences, you must link your Google AdWords account your YouTube channel.

To do this just go to the settings of your AdWords account, then choose Linked Accounts under Setup. You will then see all accounts you have linked to – Google Analytics, Google Play, Salesforce, Google Search Console, etc.

Go to the YouTube and here I have linked my channel, now click the plus, just enter a YouTube channel URL which you want to link. You will then get a link to the email related to this channel and you have to approve the linking.

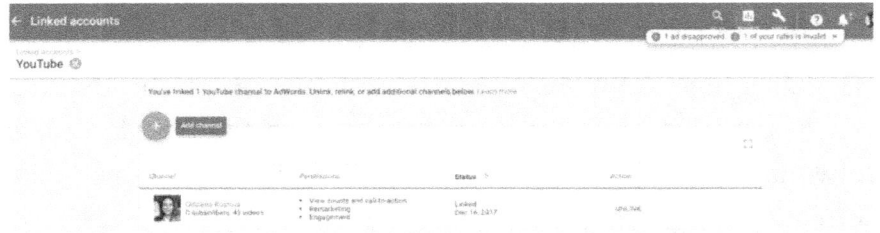

When you link your YouTube channel with your Google AdWords account you have access to target the following groups of users who:

- Viewed any video from a channel
- Viewed certain videos
- Viewed any video (as an ad) from a channel
- Viewed certain videos (as ads)
- Subscribed to a channel
- Visited a channel page
- Liked any video from a channel
- Added any video from a channel to a playlist
- Commented on any video from a channel
- Shared any video from a channel

13. CHAPTER THIRTEEN - GMAIL ADVERTISING

Gmail is arguably the biggest and best free mailbox service. It is much more than that. By creating a Gmail account, users also create a Google account and have access to any of the products Google offers. To log in YouTube you need Gmail, to use Google AdWords, Analytics, Google Play and Google maps you use the Gmail address you have created. This provides a lot of information about users' behaviour online across all Google properties.

Gmail is part of the Google Display Network and can be used to display ads in the mailbox. The ad solutions on Gmail are designed for each stage of the marketing funnel – from brand awareness to driving action.

In the chapter about GDN I explained how to set up a display campaign. There, we had an option to choose whether to set up Standard display campaign or a Gmail campaign. What is Gmail advertising? Your ads will appear in the promotional or social folder of a Gmail box on the top of all emails.

A Gmail ad looks like an email but it is not. It is actually a display ad. When you click on the Gmail ad in your inbox it expands and you can choose whether to click on it and be taken to a landing page. You can forward them to contacts, bookmark Gmail ads in your mailbox, but you cannot respond to them, because they are not really emails.

Set up a Gmail Campaign

Step 1. To set up a campaign you start like with each other type we talked about. First click on the plus button in the Campaign section in Google AdWords and select a Display campaign.

Step 2. Then choose a goal. You can only build a Gmail campaign with Sales, Leads and Website Traffic goals, or without a goal. Once you have decided, just select Create a Gmail campaign, instead of Standard Display.

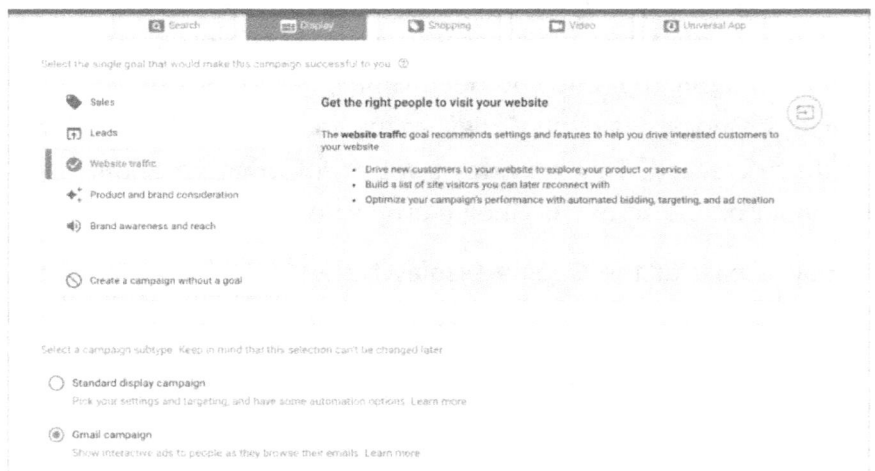

Step 3. Name your campaign, select languages and targeting locations.

Step 4. Choose the type of bidding you would like to use. With some campaign goals, there is only one option. If your goal is Sales or Leads, you can focus on Conversions or Conversion Value which corresponds to Target CPA or Target ROAS as an automated strategy. You can still set up manual bids.

If you have chosen Website Traffic as a goal, you can choose between Target CPA, Target ROAS and Maximize Clicks as automated strategies or set up manual bids.

Step 5. Choose a daily budget, ad rotation, schedule and device preferences if any.

Step 6. Select targeting for your ad group. Here, you can select from some of the targeting options available for Display and YouTube campaigns.

First, you can select keywords. Google recommends using contextual keywords like names of competitors and services like yours. The Gmail keywords are not based on the content which users look for or email about. They are like the keywords used for Display ads – based on interest users demonstrated with their online behaviour. However, these are not the same as the keywords you can use on YouTube which correspond directly to the Google Search queries users have done.

I know it sounds complicated, but to summarise it – Display and Gmail work with contextual keywords based on users' content consumption, whereas on YouTube(which is a video search engine by itself) you can target people by the keywords they have typed in on Google Search.

Next, choose audiences. You have the full assortment of audiences which you can get on a Standard Display campaign – Affinity Categories, In-Market Segments, Custom Affinity and Remarketing to web visitors. You cannot use Custom Intent, which is only for

Standard Display, but you can use Life Events, Customer Match(uploaded email list of customers) and Similar to Customer Match.

You can add another filter on top of keywords and audiences with demographics. As usually, keep an eye on the size of your audience – too many layers can reduce the people you can target significantly.

Step 7. Create a Gmail ad.

The ad creation process is very simplified from a year ago. You can create a Gmail ad directly in the interface, or upload a ready HTML coded ad. The second option gives you the opportunity to use a media type of creative, similar to a newsletter.

If you are making your Gmail ad from scratch, this is quite easy. You just have to upload an image or a video, write a headline, description and a landing page URL. You can also upload a header image as an option. In the example below, I uploaded my logo as a header.

You can include some extra bits to your ad like a Call to Action, Teaser and a customized colour. The teaser will be displayed in the email subject line and can be used to attract more clicks with a catchy offer.

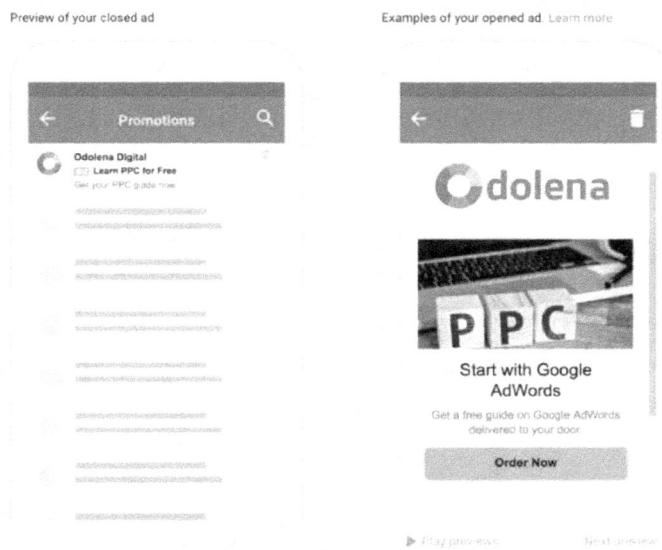

What you see above is a Gmail ad preview on a mobile. There is a reason why the mobile preview appears first – it is crucial your ad looks good on mobile as a lot of people access their email there. You can see how the ad looks in the folder and also expanded after the user has clicked on it.

If you have Google Merchant Centre account for your e-commerce, you can choose the catalogue option and add images of some of your products. They will be displayed in the expanded Gmail ad and by clicking on them users will be directed to your sales page. If you are using this format, it is recommended you use a Sales goal for your campaign.

Then you press ad to campaign, create a campaign and you are done!

FINAL WORDS

This book is meant to help someone who has none or little experience with digital marketing to understand and self-manage some of the main online channels. Becoming a master of online marketing takes some time and practice.

Keeping up with the latest technological news is crucial. During the five months I was writing this book, Google and Facebook announced numerous changes on their advertising platforms. I had to adjust the text according to the latest updates, include more ad and campaign types, even the brand name Google AdWords was changed officially to Google Ads.

Having in mind the speed of changes and development of online marketing, this book contains some of the basic knowledge which you would need to run your own campaigns. This book is in no way written to take away work from marketing agencies. After a certain stage, you will not be able to maintain your marketing yourself and it makes sense of outsourcing it to an internal team or an agency. However, in the initial stage when you are trying to evaluate your product, test your idea, or simply cannot afford paying a professional, this book comes in handy!

When you are starting up a new business, having the knowledge on how the online marketing world functions can help you validate your assumptions by running a simple and low budget campaign. This can help you prove there is interest in what you offer and apply for more funding.

If you are looking to hire an agency or marketer, knowing the basics, can help you evaluate their skill and ask relevant questions.

My mission is to educate and make online marketing accessible to as many businesses as possible. I have collected material from numerous online courses, articles and my own experience to put it in this book. I wish this is the start of your journey in digital marketing. From here, you can only upgrade our knowledge further.

If you would like to learn about the latest updates in Digital Marketing, check out my website: https://Odolena.com/ I have been posting a new article there every week for the last couple of years and I intend doing so in the future.

As a token of gratitude for reading my book, I would like to provide you with one more thing – my list of **24 Marketing Tactics to Leverage Your Business**. Here is a link for you to claim the list: http://bit.ly/2SNPb3T Add your email and I will send the list to you immediately. I always find it interesting to see how many of my readers follow through to the end of the book!

This is all from me, thank you and I wish you best of luck!

Odolena

www.ingramcontent.com/pod-product-compliance
Lightning Source LLC
Chambersburg PA
CBHW071454220526
45472CB00003B/792